This book was made possible through
the generous assistance of:

 Eastman Kodak Co.

 Merrill Lynch

 UNITED AIRLINES

 Apple Computer, Inc.

 The Hertz Corporation

Dilip Mehta

First published 1986 by Collins Publishers, New York,
London, Glasgow, Toronto, Sydney, Auckland,
Johannesburg.

Library of Congress Cataloging-in-Publication Data
Main entry under title: A Day in the Life of America

ISBN 0-00-255332-5 /Paperback ISBN: 0-00-649207-X

2. United States—Social life and customs—1971—Pic-
torial works. 3. Photography, Journalistic—United
States.
I. Smolan, Rick.
II. Cohen, David.

E169.04.D38 1986
973.927'022'2   86-17190

Project Directors: Rick Smolan and David Cohen

Art Director: Leslie Smolan

Printed in Japan   First printing August 1986

A Day in the Life of America

Photographed by 200 of the
world's leading photojournalists
on one day, May 2, 1986

Collins Publishers San Francisco

A Division of HarperCollins*Publishers*

The Sand Hills of Nebraska, 6:30 a.m.: Five-year-old
Merici Vinton sleeps securely in her parents' bed.

Charleston, South Carolina, 6:30 a.m: The Citadel's 2,000 cadets wake up to a bugler blowing reveille over the school's public-address system.

Graciela Iturbide

East Los Angeles, California, 7 a.m.: A young
Mexican-American woman named Rosario plays
with her five-month-old son Joe.

Battle Creek, Michigan, 7:30 a.m.: Sandra Carver, 18, gears up for her final month of classes at Lakeview High School. She says she can't clean up her room because she's too busy studying for final exams.

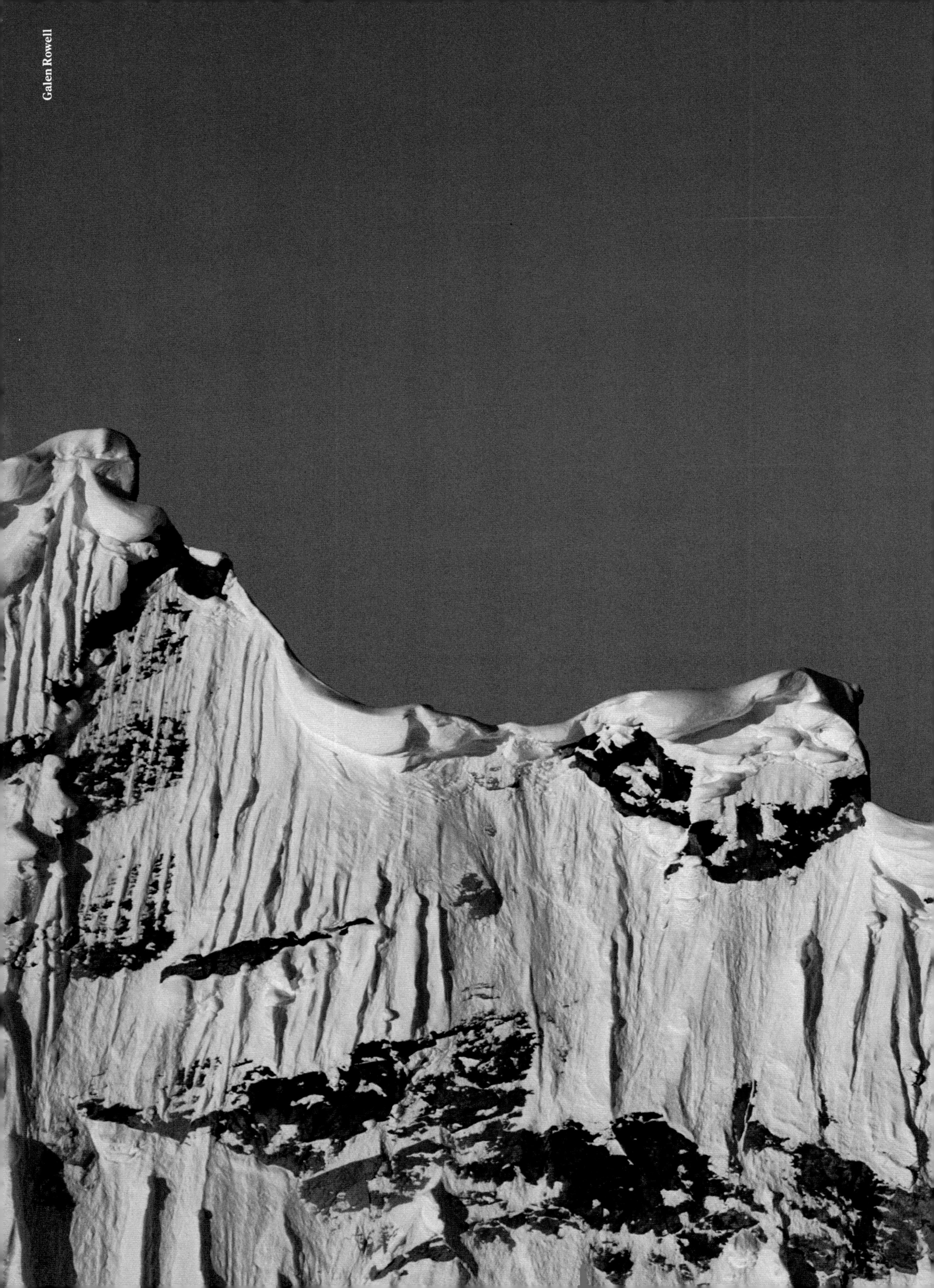

Galen Rowell

The book you are holding in your hands is a visual time capsule, an impression of life in America taken on Friday, May 2, 1986, by 200 of the world's leading photographers. No picture here is more than twenty-four hours older or younger than any other, and no picture here has been shot for any purpose other than to document the harmonies and paradoxes of life in America as it was lived on this one ordinary day.

America is a complex country and a proud one. It is an idea, a beckoning, an opportunity. It has always been an improbable country, and to set out to capture it in a single day was an improbable, some would say, impossible, idea.

A Day in the Life of America does not claim to be the true record of even one day. A day cannot be collected as it passes by in a blaze of light between shadows. Yet on May 2nd America yielded some of its secrets to these world class photographers. There are several hundred photographs here, culled from more than 235,000. But even 235,000 images barely hint at the infinite moments that passed through the hills and homes and hearts of America on that day. On May 2nd America was frozen in time and, for decades to come, our children and our children's children will look at these pages with wonder at a day when 200 photographers made time stand still.

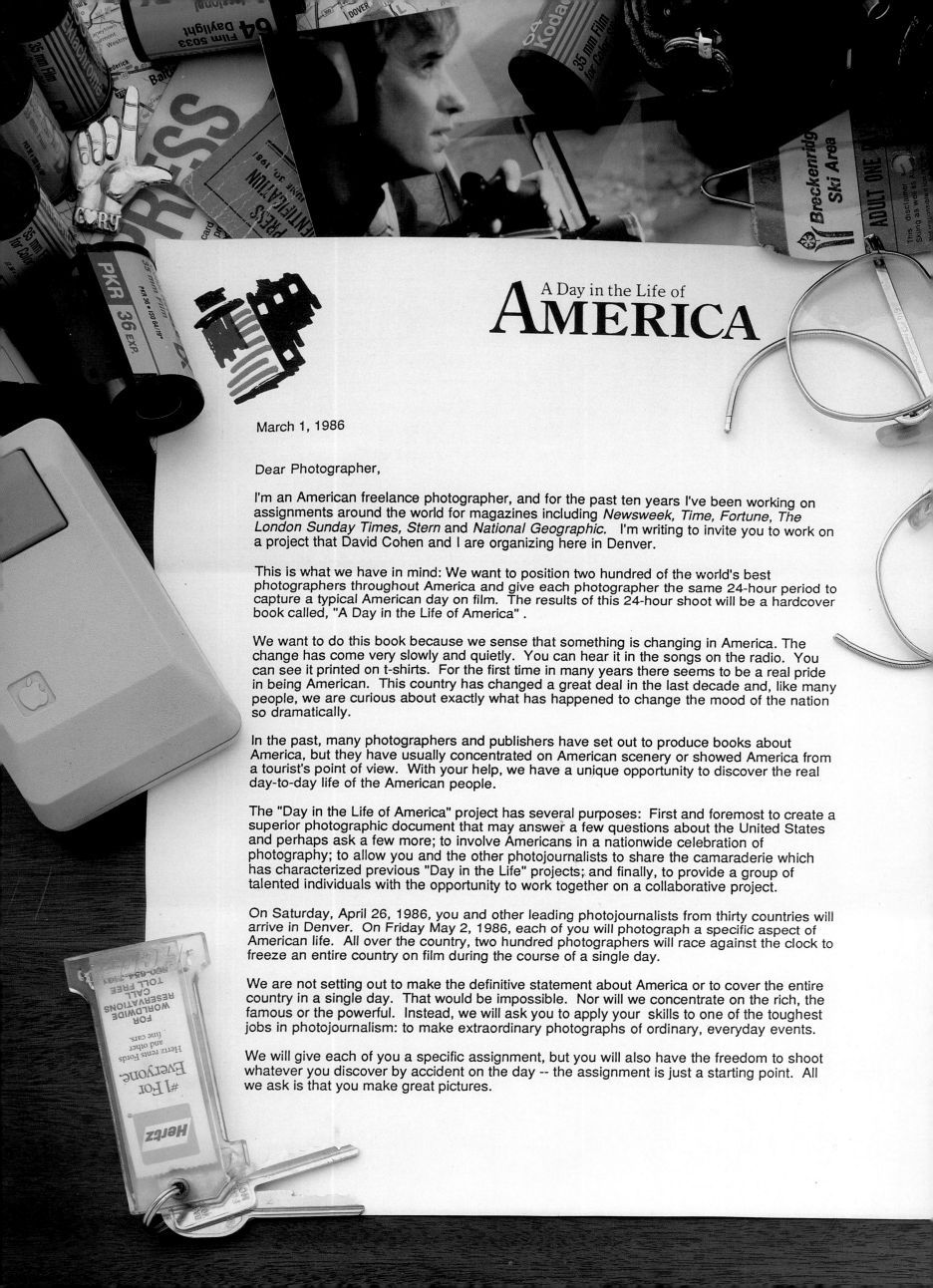

A Day in the Life of
AMERICA

March 1, 1986

Dear Photographer,

I'm an American freelance photographer, and for the past ten years I've been working on assignments around the world for magazines including *Newsweek, Time, Fortune, The London Sunday Times, Stern* and *National Geographic.* I'm writing to invite you to work on a project that David Cohen and I are organizing here in Denver.

This is what we have in mind: We want to position two hundred of the world's best photographers throughout America and give each photographer the same 24-hour period to capture a typical American day on film. The results of this 24-hour shoot will be a hardcover book called, "A Day in the Life of America" .

We want to do this book because we sense that something is changing in America. The change has come very slowly and quietly. You can hear it in the songs on the radio. You can see it printed on t-shirts. For the first time in many years there seems to be a real pride in being American. This country has changed a great deal in the last decade and, like many people, we are curious about exactly what has happened to change the mood of the nation so dramatically.

In the past, many photographers and publishers have set out to produce books about America, but they have usually concentrated on American scenery or showed America from a tourist's point of view. With your help, we have a unique opportunity to discover the real day-to-day life of the American people.

The "Day in the Life of America" project has several purposes: First and foremost to create a superior photographic document that may answer a few questions about the United States and perhaps ask a few more; to involve Americans in a nationwide celebration of photography; to allow you and the other photojournalists to share the camaraderie which has characterized previous "Day in the Life" projects; and finally, to provide a group of talented individuals with the opportunity to work together on a collaborative project.

On Saturday, April 26, 1986, you and other leading photojournalists from thirty countries will arrive in Denver. On Friday May 2, 1986, each of you will photograph a specific aspect of American life. All over the country, two hundred photographers will race against the clock to freeze an entire country on film during the course of a single day.

We are not setting out to make the definitive statement about America or to cover the entire country in a single day. That would be impossible. Nor will we concentrate on the rich, the famous or the powerful. Instead, we will ask you to apply your skills to one of the toughest jobs in photojournalism: to make extraordinary photographs of ordinary, everyday events.

We will give each of you a specific assignment, but you will also have the freedom to shoot whatever you discover by accident on the day -- the assignment is just a starting point. All we ask is that you make great pictures.

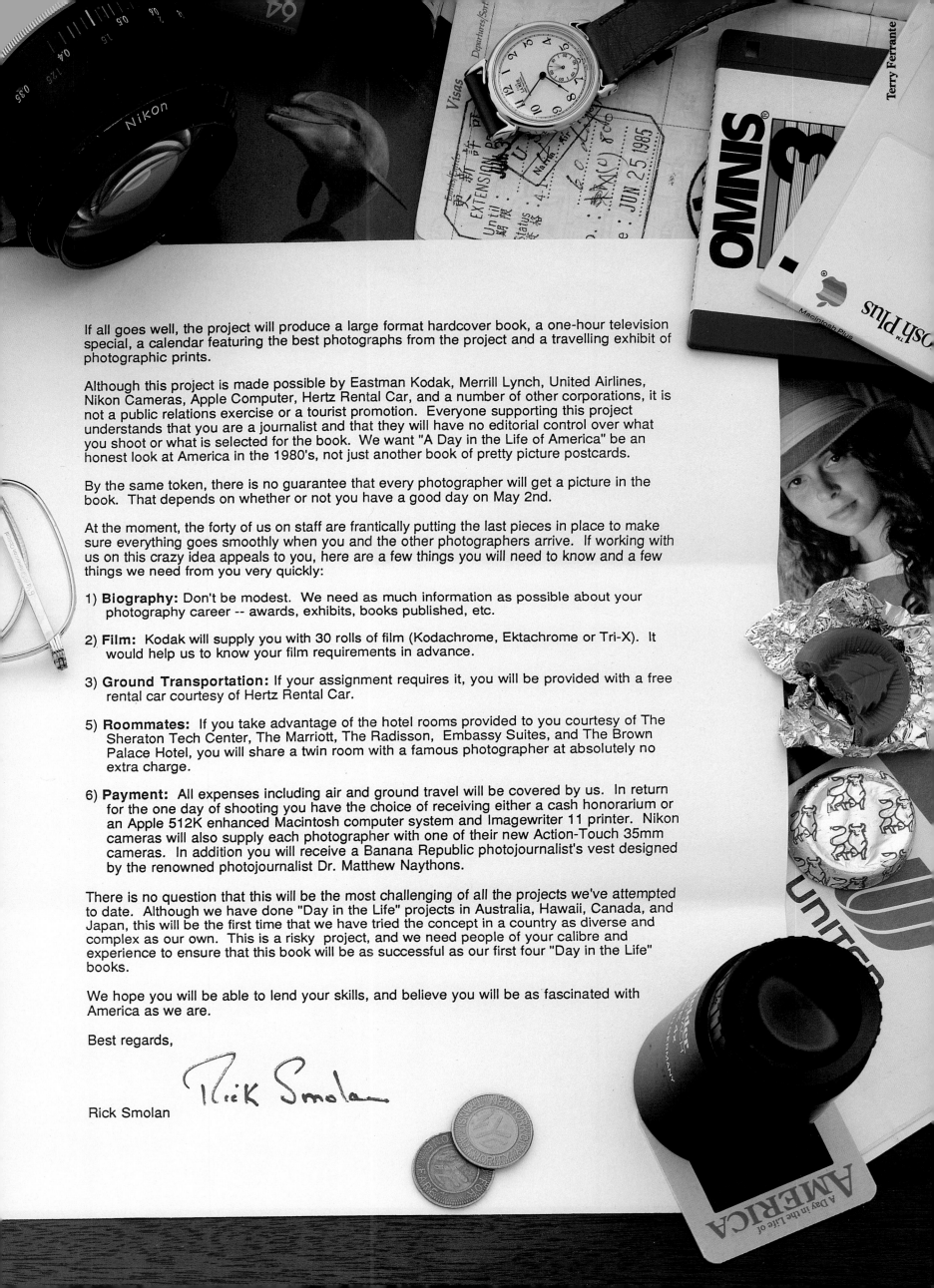

If all goes well, the project will produce a large format hardcover book, a one-hour television special, a calendar featuring the best photographs from the project and a travelling exhibit of photographic prints.

Although this project is made possible by Eastman Kodak, Merrill Lynch, United Airlines, Nikon Cameras, Apple Computer, Hertz Rental Car, and a number of other corporations, it is not a public relations exercise or a tourist promotion. Everyone supporting this project understands that you are a journalist and that they will have no editorial control over what you shoot or what is selected for the book. We want "A Day in the Life of America" be an honest look at America in the 1980's, not just another book of pretty picture postcards.

By the same token, there is no guarantee that every photographer will get a picture in the book. That depends on whether or not you have a good day on May 2nd.

At the moment, the forty of us on staff are frantically putting the last pieces in place to make sure everything goes smoothly when you and the other photographers arrive. If working with us on this crazy idea appeals to you, here are a few things you will need to know and a few things we need from you very quickly:

1) **Biography:** Don't be modest. We need as much information as possible about your photography career -- awards, exhibits, books published, etc.

2) **Film:** Kodak will supply you with 30 rolls of film (Kodachrome, Ektachrome or Tri-X). It would help us to know your film requirements in advance.

3) **Ground Transportation:** If your assignment requires it, you will be provided with a free rental car courtesy of Hertz Rental Car.

5) **Roommates:** If you take advantage of the hotel rooms provided to you courtesy of The Sheraton Tech Center, The Marriott, The Radisson, Embassy Suites, and The Brown Palace Hotel, you will share a twin room with a famous photographer at absolutely no extra charge.

6) **Payment:** All expenses including air and ground travel will be covered by us. In return for the one day of shooting you have the choice of receiving either a cash honorarium or an Apple 512K enhanced Macintosh computer system and Imagewriter 11 printer. Nikon cameras will also supply each photographer with one of their new Action-Touch 35mm cameras. In addition you will receive a Banana Republic photojournalist's vest designed by the renowned photojournalist Dr. Matthew Naythons.

There is no question that this will be the most challenging of all the projects we've attempted to date. Although we have done "Day in the Life" projects in Australia, Hawaii, Canada, and Japan, this will be the first time that we have tried the concept in a country as diverse and complex as our own. This is a risky project, and we need people of your calibre and experience to ensure that this book will be as successful as our first four "Day in the Life" books.

We hope you will be able to lend your skills, and believe you will be as fascinated with America as we are.

Best regards,

Rick Smolan

● *Previous pages 16-17*

Artistic plowman Stanley James Herd touches up his third major work, a 20-acre still-life of sunflowers near Eudora, Kansas. Herd's pallet includes rich Kansas earth, clover, alfalfa and grass. His last project was a 160-acre portrait of cowboy philosopher Will Rogers.
Photographer:
Georg Gerster, Switzerland

● *Previous page*

National Park Service workers prepare for the more than 11,000 tourists who visited the Lincoln Memorial on May 2nd.
Photographer:
Seny Norasingh, Laos

● *Above*

White-collar warriors wait for the New Haven line's commuter special in the affluent New York suburb of Greenwich, Connecticut. Midtown Manhattan's Grand Central Station is 11 stops and 52 minutes away.
Photographer:
Nicole Bengiveno, USA

● *Right*

Housewife and part-time professional ski instructor Pat Ganter holds a morning meeting with her year-old sheep dog, Contessa, at her home in Traverse City, Michigan.
Photographer:
José Azel, USA

Climbing instructor Joseph Lentini faces 80-mile-per-hour winds and a minus 40 degree wind-chill factor as he starts a four-mile walk down Lionshead Trail from the weather station at the summit of New Hampshire's Mount Washington.

Pulitzer Prize-winning photographer Jay Dickman of Dallas, Texas, reports that five minutes after he stepped outside the weather station, every one of his cameras had completely iced over. It took Dickman two hours to take his cameras apart and de-ice them. He then wrapped all of his equipment in plastic bags, went back outside and only unwrapped each camera long enough to take a picture. Dickman says, "I'd always heard about this mountain and how dangerous it's supposed to be in the winter. Now I can see why over a hundred people have been killed up there."

Photographer:
Jay Dickman, USA

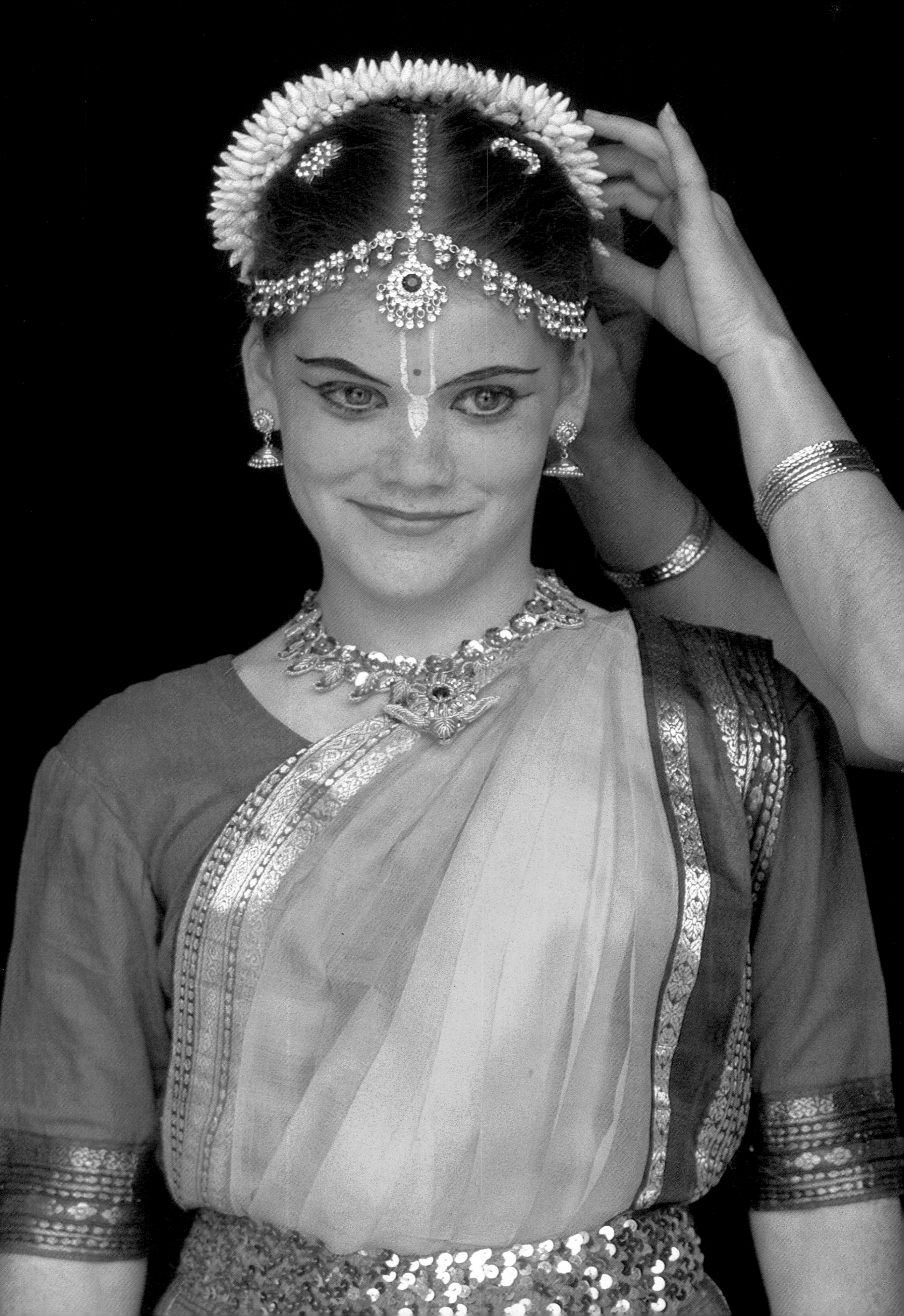

Pascal Maitre

● *Previous page*

Prabhupada's Palace of Gold, named for the founder of the Hare Krishna movement, is a showcase ''spiritual community'' built by the International Society for Krishna Consciousness on a mountaintop near Moundsville, West Virginia. On May 2nd, 13-year-old Veena Dasi (formerly Renee Walker), whose family is among the temple's 600 mostly American-born residents, gets some help from teacher Jatila Devi before joining a performance of the Bharatanatyam, a classical Indian dance.

Photographer:
Pascal Maitre, France

• *Left*

Some might call it paradise, but more than 400 members of the Havasupai tribe of American Indians just call it home. The ''Blue-Green-Water People,'' as their name translates, have been living at the bottom of the Grand Canyon for more than 1,000 years. Supai, the reservation's only town, sees a steady stream of sturdy visitors willing to make the ten-mile, five-hour trek down from the canyon rim, 5,000 feet above. (The tribe collects $9 per person per night for a camping permit plus a $10 entrance fee.) One reason for the tourist influx is Havasu Falls, just downstream from the town—also a favorite with this group of Havasupai school kids.
Photographer:
Rich Clarkson, USA

• *Above*

Nine-month-old Annalee Plant takes her morning bath in an antique English tub at the Manti House Inn, a six-room bed-and-breakfast in Manti, Utah. Her mother, Teresa, is a part-owner.
Photographer:
Michele Cardon, USA

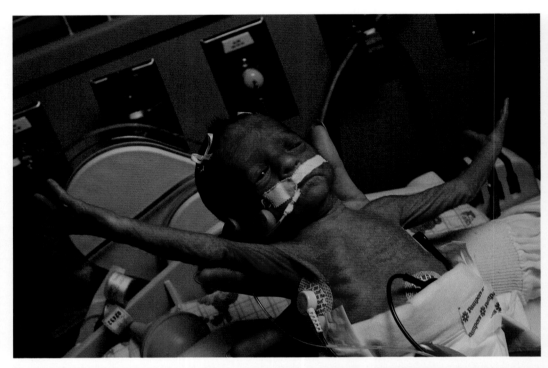

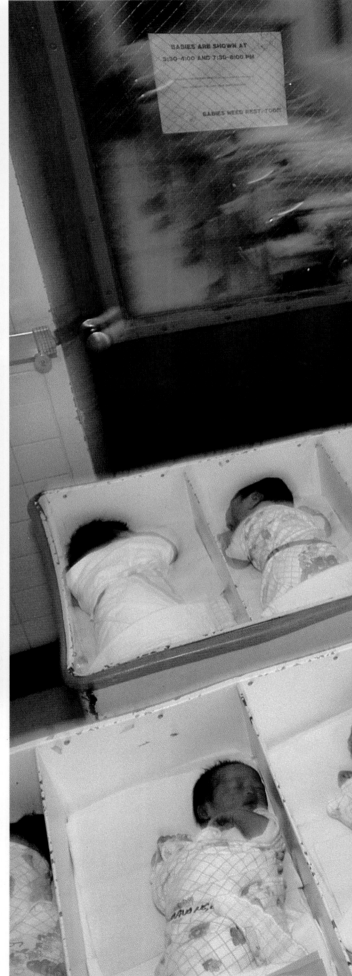

● *Above, top*

Tracy Martinez was born eight weeks premature at Dallas' Parkland Memorial Hospital. At the time of birth, Tracy weighed only 2 lbs., 12 ozs. and was 15 inches long. A week later, on May 2nd, Tracy's lungs were still too undeveloped to breathe un-aided, and she was taking oxygen and formula through tubes.
Photographer:
Barry Lewis, Britain

● *Above*

After leading a ten-member surgi-cal team through a seven-and-a-half-hour artificial heart implant and a six-hour heart and lung transplant, Dr. Bartley P. Griffith falls asleep in the surgeons' lounge at Presbyterian-University Hospital in Pittsburgh. Dr. Griffith's team has performed over 35 heart-lung transplants, helping to make Pittsburgh one of the organ transplant capitals of the world.
Photographer:
Serge Cohen, France

● *Right*

Newborn babies are carted through Parkland Memorial Hospital in Dallas four times a day to visit their parents. On average one baby is born every half hour at Parkland, the third highest birthrate of any hospital in the country.
Photographer:
Barry Lewis, Britain

● *Following page*

Lighter-than-air enthusiasts from across the Pacific Northwest take off in Walla Walla, Washington, during the 1986 Balloon Stampede. Most of the pack returned to earth an hour later five miles away. A typical hot-air rig costs about $20,000.

Photographer:

Steve Ringman, USA

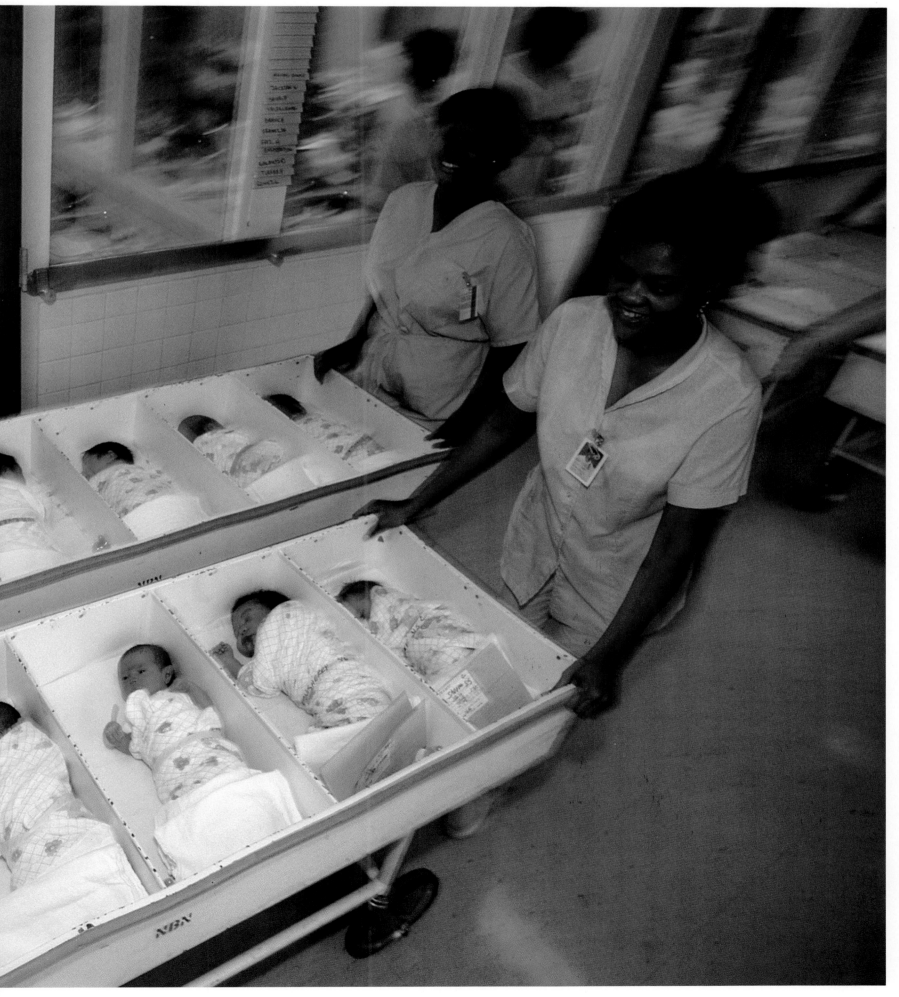

Mexico City-based photographer Graciela Iturbide spent May 2nd with a group of East Los Angeles *cholos*—a loose term for the small fringe of tough, street-wise young Mexican-Americans, mostly U.S. born—who see themselves at odds with both Anglo society and Hispanic tradition. As Iturbide explains, her subjects—members of a *cholo* street gang—were unusual in another way:

"Arturo, Lisa, Rosario and five-month-old Joe live together in the White Fence *barrio* of East L.A. Except for the baby, all are deaf-mutes. Joe is Rosario's baby, but since none of the group has a job now, they all take care of him. They spend a lot of time in their room together and driving around in their car with the baby looking for friends. Each has a nickname. Arturo is called 'Chango.' Lisa is 'Bad Girl,' and Rosario is 'Smiley.' Rosario calls her baby 'El Boo Boo.'

Photographer:
Graciela Iturbide, Mexico

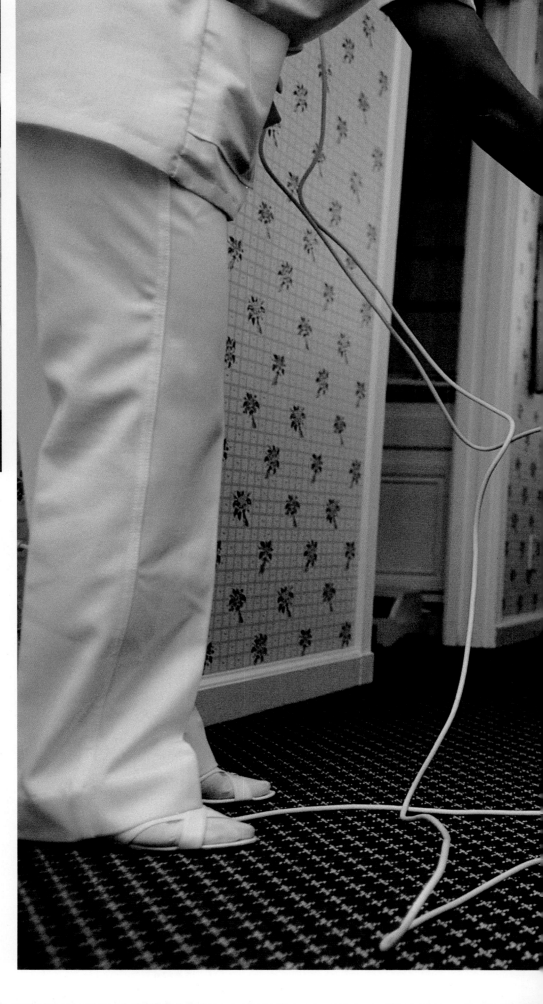

● *Above*

An Albuquerque, New Mexico, businessman simultaneously pursues high finance with *The Wall Street Journal* and low blood pressure on an exercise cycle at a local health club.

Photographer:

Arthur Grace, USA

● *Right*

At home in the Bel Air section of Los Angeles, Daniel Rosenbloom, two, helps his nanny vacuum his sister's bedroom. Daniel's father is an investor.

Photographer:

George Steinmetz, USA

On May 2nd, 2,000 traders, brokers, clerks and messengers assembled on the main trading floor of the New York Stock Exchange for a first-ever group portrait. Neal Slavin, the world's leading group portrait photographer, and four assistants spent three days planning the shot and 15 hours setting up banks of Tekno Balcar strobe lights and three synchronized cameras. Then they were given only 30 seconds to take the picture.

Slavin says, "I only had time for two exposures, so the pressure was really on. I pushed the button, and there was a loud pop as 75,000 watt-seconds of light flashed across the floor of the exchange. The equipment worked, and I breathed a huge sigh of relief."

Photographer:
Neal Slavin, USA

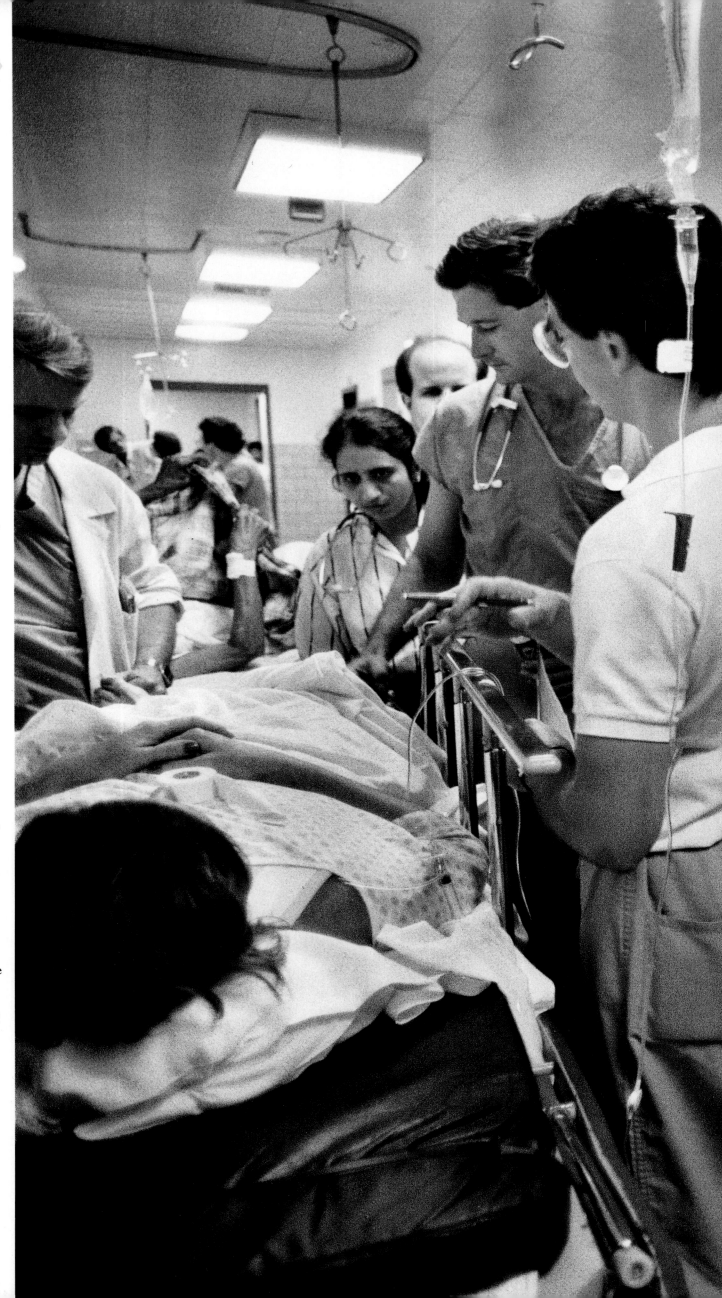

On May 2nd, the embattled emergency staff at New Orleans' 250-year-old Charity Hospital dealt with one new case every four minutes. According to Director of Operations Jim Meade, the doctors and nurses at one of America's busiest public hospitals have not had a raise in four years.

Photographer Andy Levin was dismayed by the misery he photographed on May 2nd, but impressed by the dedication of the hospital staff. Levin says, "I would not do this assignment again. It was just too intense. Having to work with people who are in pain, asking them to let me take their picture and sign releases in a matter-of-fact way was hard, even though everyone was very responsive.

"Here is what most of us would consider a snake pit of a hospital, yet if you look at the care these doctors and nurses are giving people, you would have to say they are doing a good job under tough conditions. In the long term, these people, many of them poor, were well taken care of. The only question is, how long can the staff keep it up?"

Photographer:
Andy Levin, USA

● *Below*

Why would anyone need an ultraviolet tanning bed in sun-drenched Albuquerque, New Mexico? "Because everyone works all day and no one has time to sit in the sun," says Barry Lehane, general manager of Nautilus of New Mexico.
Photographer:
Arthur Grace, USA

● *Right*

Jenny Hope slides into a tub of volcanic mud at Nance's Hot Springs in Calistoga, California. The hot springs have been owned by the Hughes family for more than 50 years. Debbie Hughes says, "The mud removes toxins from your system, relaxes your body and makes your skin real soft."
Photographer:
Wilbur E. Garrett, USA

● *Above*

The Ciemniak family meat store has been serving up homemade *kielbasa* on Joseph Campau street in Hamtramck, Michigan, since 1921.

For generations, Polish immigrants have beaten a path to the inner-city Detroit enclave—and high-paying assembly-line jobs in the nearby auto plants. In recent years, however, many of their children and grandchildren have moved to the suburbs, and Hamtramck's newest arrivals include Yugoslavs, Czechs and other Eastern Europeans.
Photographer:
Dennis Chamberlin, USA

● *Right*

On May 2nd, waitress Emma Maison contends with some of the nearly 1,900 kosher breakfasts served to guests at the Concord Hotel in the Catskill Mountains. The Concord, a sprawling resort on the shores of Kiamesha Lake, caters mostly to Jewish families from the New York City area.
Photographer:
Victor Fisher, Canada

● *Following page*

In Boonville, Missouri, members of the Kemper Military School and College swim team line up in Johnston Field House. Kemper was founded in 1844, and its graduates first fought for the South during the War Between the States.
Photographer:
Nina Barnett, USA

Nina Barnett

● *Left*

Eileen Slocum lives year-round in a mansion built by her aunt, Georgette Brown, in 1894. Her home is one of the largest ''cottages'' in the old-line summer resort of Newport, Rhode Island. A direct descendent of Roger Williams, who founded the state in 1636, Mrs. Slocum and her husband, John, a retired diplomat, have 11 grandchildren. Her chef, Carlos Juarez, worked in the Washington embassy of his native Argentina until its ambassador was recalled during the 1982 Falkland Islands War.

Photographer:

Michael O'Brien, USA

● *Above*

In downtown Philadephia's Reading Terminal Market, James Jackson offers a complete menu of shoe shines. The mural behind customers David O'Neil and Thomas Dramis is modeled on John Trumbull's 18th-century painting that depicts the signing of the Declaration of Independence in nearby Independence Hall. Thanks to a carefully planned renovation, the sprawling Reading Terminal, once a fading commuter rail stop, has taken on a new shine of its own.

Photographer:

Patrick Ward, Britain

● *Following page*

Flesh and bones: On May 2nd, model Larry Gilkes was one of two possible subjects at an illustration class at New York City's Fashion Institute of Technology.

Photographer:

Burk Uzzle, USA

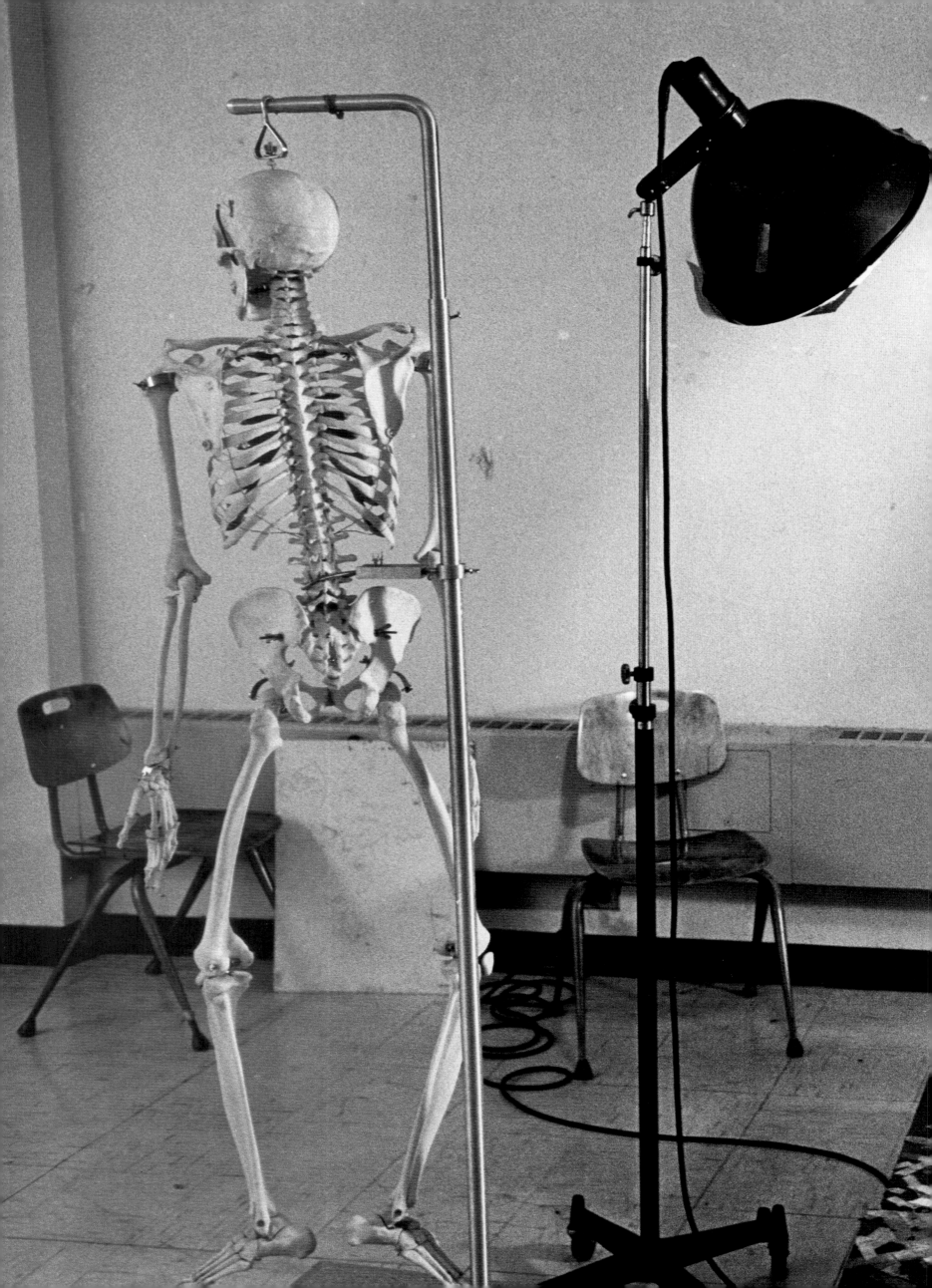

Burk Uzzle.

● *Left*

It took sculptor Gutzon Borglum 14 years and a lot of dynamite to carve Mount Rushmore National Memorial into the granite of southwestern South Dakota. On May 2nd, photographer J. P. Laffont climbed up for a closer look at Thomas Jefferson and Abraham Lincoln.

Photographer:

Jean-Pierre Laffont, France

● *Above*

Guy and Margaret Holtzapple of York, Pennsylvania, enjoy the sun outside the Heritage Grand Hotel in Ft. Mill, South Carolina. Guy, a maintenance worker at York's Bonton department store, and Margaret, a machine operator, have been married for nearly 45 years.

Photographer:

Jerry Valente, USA

Odessa, Texas　　　　　　　　　**Andrew Stawicki**

Juneau, Alaska　　　　　　　　　**Donna Ferrato**

New York, New York　　　　　　　　　**Ralph Ginzberg**

New York, New York   Bill Pierce   Santa Fe, New Mexico   Arnaud de Wildenberg

Cabin Creek, West Virginia   James L. Stanfield

53

From the top of a manure pile at Hitch Feeders in Garden City, Kansas, a feedlot cowboy can survey 50,000 cattle having their last super-fattening supper before the final roundup. Trucked in from ranches across the country, the Angus, Hereford and Charlois steers chew their way through 370 tons of high-moisture Kansas feed corn each day.

Weighing in at around 700 pounds the day they walk in, the animals bulk up to nearly 1,100 pounds in just under four months. Then they are moved to holding pens (*following page*) at nearby Val-Agri Meat Packing Plant. An average of 2,800 cattle a day spend two or three hours in the pens before trundling off to the slaughterhouse, where they are stunned with high-voltage electricity, killed by a single bullet in the head and then carved up by teams of butchers using power saws. In 1985, Val-Agri, one of the country's top packers, shipped 831 million pounds of dressed beef—almost enough for one quarter-pound hamburger for every person on earth.

Photographer:
Chris Johns, USA

● *Above*

Driving towards the Chisos Mountains in Big Bend National Park, Texas.
Photographer:
Tom Zetterstrom, USA

● *Right*

Cat owner Ginger Cantacessi posted a homemade warning to vehicles passing her Golden Valley, Nevada, home. Here she poses with Sylvia, one of her four cats.
Photographer:
Dana Fineman, USA

● *Following page*

The northbound Evanston Express waits to cross the Lake Street line in Chicago's downtown ''Loop.'' The 215 miles of Chicago Transit Authority track —usually called the ''el'' for its many elevated sections—carries half a million riders daily.
Photographer:
Francoise Huguier, France

DANGER
ELECTRIC CURRENT
DO NOT GO DOWN
TO TRACK

Nashville, Tennessee

Tsuneo Enari, Japan

NO EATING OR DRINKING IN THIS CAR

NOTICE TO PASSENGERS
THIS VEHICLE AND ITS DRIVER ARE LICENSED BY THE NEW YORK CITY TAXI AND LIMOUSINE COMMISSION. ANY COMPLAINTS CONCERNING THE DRIVER AND/OR VEHICLE SHOULD BE DIRECTED TO THE COMMISSION - 221 WEST 41 ST. NEW YORK, N.Y. 10036 **PHONE - (212)382-9301**

THANK YOU FOR NOT SMOKING

INCREASED TAXI FARE
Effective 12:01 A.M. July 15, 1984 the initial drop on the meter will increase from $1.00 to $1.10. The mileage charge will remain the same. The Driver is authorized to collect this 10¢ additional per trip charge until the meter has been recalibrated to reflect $1.10 as the initial drop.

NEWARK INTERNATIONAL AIRPORT PASSENGERS
Effective November 6, 1983, the rate of fare for trips to NEWARK INTERNATIONAL AIRPORT from anywhere in the five boroughs of New York City shall be the amount indicated on the meter plus $10.00 and tolls.
NYC TAXI & LIMOUSINE COMMISSION
JAY L. TUROFF, CHAIRMAN
Complaint Phone #869-4237

THE LAW ...SENGERS **MUST** ...E CURB SIDE ...OORS ONLY

NO **U** TURNS PERMITTED BY ORDER OF N.Y.C. POLICE DEPT.

REMINDER TAKE YOUR PROPERTY
POLICE DEPARTMENT   CITY OF NEW YORK

PLEA...

DRIVER NOT REQUIRED TO CHANGE BILL OVER $10

New York, New York

Joy Wolf, USA

Charles F. "Andy" Anderson goes to church every morning at 7:30, then hits the streets of Reno, Nevada, to campaign against abortion. "I served 20 years in the military," he says, "and I didn't fight so hard as I'm doing now. There's a hidden World War III against the unborn that's going to explode one day. People say I'm crazy and I say, 'Yes, I'm crazy about life.'"

Photographer Dana Fineman says, "I met Anderson in front of his house, and he told me that he was going to pray. I thought, 'Good, I'll get some pictures here.' He got on his knees, and I started to make my shots. After about 15 minutes, I was finished, and I said, 'OK, Andy, I got it. That's enough.' But he wouldn't stop. He just stayed on his knees for another half hour praying and praying for the souls of the unborn."

Photographer:
Dana Fineman, USA

Chief Justice of the United States Warren E. Burger works on an opinion in his Supreme Court chambers in Washington, D.C.

Photographer Brian Lanker found the Chief Justice in a cooperative mood. Lanker says, "The Chief Justice was certainly conscious of his image, but he was relaxed enough to really work with me. He joked with my daughter, Jackie, who was assisting me, and I found him to be a very nice person. Gracious and, as everyone says, he certainly looks the role of the Chief Justice. People say the Supreme Court is a tough place to shoot, but I thought it was a breath of fresh air compared with the White House [*see following page*]."

The Chief Justice's light mood was surprising considering what he must have had on his mind. Less than a month after Lanker's session with America's 15th Chief Justice, Burger resigned his seat on the Court.

Photographer:
Brian Lanker, USA

It usually costs $5 to have your picture taken with this life-size cutout of Ronald Reagan at Union Station in Indianapolis. But the teenage entrepreneurs who run the concession let Australian photographer John Marmaras snap passers-by for free.

Photographer:
John Marmaras, Australia

The First Dog: Rex, a one-year-old Cavalier King Charles Spaniel, was presented to Mrs. Reagan by the President in 1985.

Pulitzer Prize winner Brian Lanker decided to make a portrait of America's top dog when he found out that he was not allowed to take photographs of much else in the executive mansion. Most photographers who shoot in official situations have gripes about access. Here is what Lanker had to say: "I was promised complete access, but I found out that the open doors of the White House were closed. Things soon became absurd. I couldn't photograph the gardeners on the South Lawn because they were in a security detail. I couldn't photograph Rex getting a shampoo because that was on the second level, which was private. I couldn't photograph the mess hall because people don't look good when they are eating. I couldn't photograph the people in the kitchen because they were Navy personnel, and some people might not like the fact that taxpayers are paying for Navy personnel to fix the food in the White House. In short, there was no access to speak of."

Photographer:
Brian Lanker, USA

A senior cadet at The Citadel in Charleston, South Carolina, pulled freshmen Paul Calcagno and Christopher Chope out of a morning line-up to demonstrate traditional ''bracing.'' Says *Day in the Life of America* photographer Aaron Chang, ''It's an extreme form of coming to attention that they make the freshmen do. They have to touch their shoulder blades together and bury their chins into their chests.''

Chang, who is best known for his work as a surfing photographer, found it difficult to ''infiltrate'' a military academy. ''I'm not really familiar with the military. I've never had any experience with them. What I had to do was win the trust of the cadets in a very short period of time. Relating to a military cadet is almost the opposite of relating to a surfer. It was really hard to get these guys to open up.''

Photographer:
Aaron Chang, USA

● *Left*

Twenty thousand new "leather-necks" endure three grueling months of "boot camp" each year at the U.S. Marine Corps Recruit Depot in Parris Island, South Carolina. On May 2nd, *Day in the Life of America* photographer Frank Johnston, a 1963 Marine Corps recruit, went back for a visit: "One of the most amazing scenes," Johnston says, "is the gas chamber. They use a sort of pepper gas, and at first the recruits have their gas masks on. Then they make them take the masks off, and stay in there for ten or fifteen seconds. When they come out, the drill instructors make them walk around on the grass until they recover."

Photographer:
Frank Johnston, USA

● *Above*

Air Force Capt. Keith Davis and Lt. Patrick Ide run through their monthly four-hour brush-up session in a missile-procedures trainer at Minot Air Force Base in North Dakota. The trainer is an exact duplicate of the 15 underground launch control centers attached to Minot's 150 Minuteman nuclear missile silos.

If the President were to order a nuclear attack, here is what would happen: A launch order would come over the phone and via telex printout. Captain Davis and Lt. Ide would remove the launch codes and keys from a locked safe with two separate combinations. (Davis and Ide each know only one combination.) Then, each would enter one set of codes and simultaneously turn the keys. By turning their keys for five seconds, Davis and Ide together cast one "launch vote." (Their key-holes are 12 feet apart so that neither can cast a launch vote on his own.) When the computer receives two launch votes from two separate locations, the nuclear missiles are fired.

Crew members are seated in special chairs that roll on tracks along banks of computers and communications equipment. They are buckled in to help cushion the shock waves from an incoming nuclear warhead.

Photographer:
Joe McNally, USA

Aaron Chang

● *Previous pages 74-75*

The Second Battalion, South Carolina Corps of Cadets, forms up for Friday dress parade in its quadrangle at The Citadel. The cadets' uniforms are essentially unchanged from those worn when the military college was founded in Charleston in 1842.
Photographer:
Aaron Chang, USA

● *Previous page*

Jane and her husband, Michael, in their Brooklyn, New York, apartment: Jane, who is discussing the day's shooting schedule, is better known to millions of adult-film fans as ''Veronica Hart.''
Photographer:
William Albert Allard, USA

● *Above*

More than 40,000 people a day walk, jog and bicycle through New York City's 113-year-old Central Park. On May 2nd, two of Manhattan's senior citizens rested on a park bench during a springtime stroll.
Photographer:
Dilip Mehta, Canada

● *Right*

Edmund P. and Ephraim N. Lowe do pretty much everything the same way. The 63-year-old twins, both bachelors, work together as surveyors and have lived with their 87-year-old mother in the same house for the past 48 years (except for World War II, when they both went off to Europe— together as usual—with the Army Air Corps). Afternoons they usually stop by for coffee and Cokes at Smitty's Restaurant in their hometown of Oxford, Mississippi.
Photographer:
Alain Nogues, France

Just inside the U.S. border, two young Mexicans wait for their chance to sprint 200 yards past Immigration and Naturalization Service (INS) patrols and into a south El Paso *barrio*.

During all of 1960, agents working the U.S. Border Patrol's 341-mile El Paso sector apprehended 3,648 illegal aliens crossing the Rio Grande River from Mexico. During the first week of May 1986, alone, El Paso agents caught nearly twice that number.

This huge migration, spurred in part by economic crisis south of the border, has created a sad game of cat-and-mouse along the banks of the Rio Grande.

Photographer:
Larry Price, USA

For illegal aliens or *indocumentados*, the first part of the trip is relatively easy. Border Patrol agents around El Paso use cameras and electronic sensors to detect illegal aliens crossing the river, but they long ago gave up trying to close the many holes that have been cut in the chain-link fence lining the U.S. side. From the fence it is still a long sprint to El Paso itself, across rail yards and dusty fields where Border Patrol agents in vans, four-wheel-drive vehicles and on foot form the only real line of defense. On most mornings, several hundred hopeful job-seekers gather near the fence. Then they wait for the right moment and take their chances.

Photographer:
Larry Price, USA

● *Left*

Although most illegal aliens from Mexico are young men, many are part of the so-called ''maid brigade''—women with regular jobs as domestics in El Paso.

They often use the services of a *guía* to get across the 70-yard-wide riverbed. (Usual fee: $1 per trip.)

Photographer:
Larry Price, USA

● *Below*

By INS estimates, only one in three illegal border-crossers in the El Paso sector is unlucky enough to be caught and taken to the holding cells in the agency's nearby Processing Center. All except non-Mexicans (less than one percent of the total) and attempted drug smugglers are bused back to Mexico, in most cases having spent no more than two hours in the U.S. Virtually all will try to cross the border again.

Photographer:
Larry Price, USA

● *Right*

At home in El Paso, 10-year-old Erika Trujillo watches as her father Alfonso gets ready for his busy midnight-to-eight a.m. shift as a Border Patrol Agent.

Photographer:
Larry Price, USA

Big Mountain Navajo Reservation, Arizona **April Saul**

Los Angeles, California **David Hume Kennerly**

Natchez, Mississippi **Jay Maise**

Atlantic City, New Jersey   R. Ian Lloyd

San Francisco, California   Yan Morvan

Telluride, Colorado   Eddie Adams

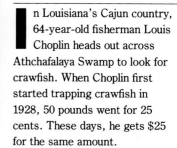

In Louisiana's Cajun country, 64-year-old fisherman Louis Choplin heads out across Athchafalaya Swamp to look for crawfish. When Choplin first started trapping crawfish in 1928, 50 pounds went for 25 cents. These days, he gets $25 for the same amount.

In his long lifetime, Choplin has been a fisherman, a trapper, a soldier (he took part in the D-Day invasion of Normandy), a chef, a lumberjack, a butcher, a painter, a carpenter, a pipeline foreman and, yes, a volunteer Santa Claus at a local institute for the mentally retarded. Now, Choplin "lives in the swamp" with Gleanor, his wife of 41 years, and one of his four children. He crawfishes year-round and traps fur in the winter.

Photographer:
Matthew Naythons, USA

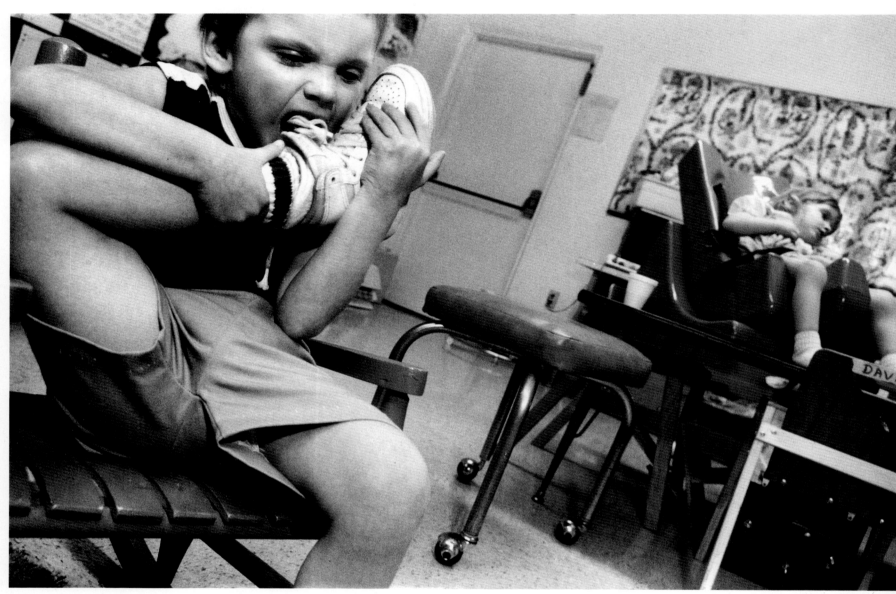

●*Previous page*

Temperate sea mists have nurtured this stand of *sequoia sempervirens* since Ghengis Khan started his march across Asia in the 13th century. The largest of these redwoods—located in 550-acre Muir Woods National Monument near San Francisco—top 250 feet in height and 13 feet in diameter.

Photographer:

Robert Azzi, USA

●*Above*

At the Upper Pinellas Association for Retarded Citizens (UPARC) training facility in Clearwater, Florida, five-year-old Patrick persists in using his teeth to untie his shoes. Normal at birth, he was blinded and severely brain-damaged by a high fever in 1985. In the background is three-year-old Michelle, one of seven other children in the group.

Photographer:

Mary Ellen Mark, USA

●*Right*

UPARC group home manager Anne Marvel helps 25-year-old Caren (who suffers from Down's syndrome) to get ready for a party at the residence. Marvel says, "Caren can't arrange her hair and make-up herself, but when we're finished, she knows that she looks pretty, and she smiles. That makes my job here worthwhile. It's emotionally exhausting, but the rewards outweigh the frustrations, and at the end of the day I'm left with a good feeling inside."

Photographer:

Mary Ellen Mark, USA

● *Left, top*

When southern California's hot spring sun became too oppressive, this Beverly Hills lady popped into Saks to buy a new sun hat.
Photographer:
George Steinmetz, USA

● *Left, bottom*

There's almost always a waiting line for swimming pool blackjack at the Tropicana Hotel in Las Vegas, Nevada. In deference to the location, the tabletop is nylon instead of regulation green felt; a special heater behind the dealer dries out damp hundred-dollar bills.
Photographer:
Francois Robert, Switzerland

● *Below*

Water-exercise class meets three times a week in the pool at the Top of the World retirement community in Clearwater, Florida.
Photographer:
Mary Ellen Mark, USA

Above

● *Above*

● *Left*

Doorman Michael Canavan checks the time outside the Fifth Avenue branch of Gucci, internationally renowned purveyors of leather goods, handbags, fashions and accessories. The New York store's least expensive item, a Gucci keyring, costs $20. The dearest is an 18 carat Marquis cut canary diamond ring, available for a cool $345,000.
Photographer:
Jodi Cobb, USA

● *Left*

Mary Cassell Johns Bernard considers a new evening outfit at Jack Krawcheck's for Women in her hometown of Charleston, South Carolina.
Photographer:
Aaron Chang, USA

● *Left*

American designer Norma Kamali's fall '86 line debuts for the fashion press at her midtown boutique on West 56th Street in Manhattan.
Photographer:
Jodi Cobb, USA

Photographer David Turnley—
just back from the front lines of
South Africa's racial turmoil—
made this May 2nd portrait
through the window of a parked
car on New York's 125th Street—
Main Street of Harlem, U.S.A.

Photographer:
David Turnley, USA

● *Previous pages 102-103*

Laura Dickey, 77, and Charles Kenyon, 78, play bride and groom during the mock wedding portion of a senior citizen fashion show in Fairlee, Vermont. An unconfirmed rumor has it that, back in the 1920s, Miss Dickey had a little crush on Mr. Kenyon.

Photographer:

Christopher Pillitz, Britain

● *Previous page*

Robert Mondavi, one of America's best-known vintners, and his wife, Margrit Biever, like their privacy—which may explain why the couple's two-year-old, multimillion-dollar house in California's Napa Valley has an indoor swimming pool but only one bedroom.

Photographer:

Wilbur E. Garrett, USA

● *Above*

On May 2nd, Ronald Reagan was traveling in the Far East, but Vice President of the United States George Bush was on hand in the White House to welcome Cassie Camp Plunkett of Porum, Oklahoma, who celebrated her 100th birthday on March 15th.

Photographer:

Brian Lanker, USA

● *Right*

Photographer Vladimir Sichov left the U.S.S.R. in 1979, smuggling out 180,000 photographs—later widely published in the West—depicting hidden aspects of Soviet life. On May 2, 1986, near Rockefeller Center in midtown Manhattan, he found one of New York City's estimated 60,000 homeless men and women begging on a busy street corner. "I did those pictures in Russia," he says, "I do the same thing here."

Photographer:

Vladimir Sichov, Stateless

● *Following page*

Havana is 225 miles away, but daily lunch at her Uncle Antonio's is still an old-fashioned family affair for Miami attorney Maria Elena Prio (center), a leading figure in the city's 700,000-strong Cuban community. Her late father, Carlos Prio Socarras, was Cuba's last president before dictator Fulgencio Batista took over in 1952.

Photographer:

Stephanie Maze, USA

● *Left*

The Wagon Wheel Cafe is the center of small town life in Cuba, Kansas. The "menu" next to waitress Anna Kauer is a brownie which stayed in the oven a bit too long.

Photographer:

Jim Richardson, USA

● *Above*

William Banyard, age 20 months, is not quite sure about the driving conditions at Mike Pompa's barbershop, where most Greenwich, Connecticut, kids get their first haircut.

Photographer:

Nicole Bengiveno, USA

● *Left*

Yvonne Mitchell, 19, lives with her four-month-old son, Harry Simpson Jr., in North Lawndale, on Chicago's tough West Side. "There are some positive things happening in North Lawndale," says photographer Bruce Talamon. "I tried very hard to find them, but it was tough."

Photographer:
Bruce Talamon, USA

● *Above*

May 2nd was a big day for the Morgan family of Harlow, England. They were headed for a Hawaiian vacation aboard United Airlines Flight 1 out of Chicago.

Photographer Douglas Kirkland also had a big day. His assignment was to shoot America's first sunrise over Maine's Mount Katahdin (see page 1) and sunset the same day over Maui. He was halfway to Hawaii when he made this picture.

Photographer:
Douglas Kirkland, Canada

● *Left*

Yvonne Mitchell, 19, lives with
her four-month-old son, Harry
Simpson Jr., in North Lawndale,
on Chicago's tough West Side.
''There are some positive things
happening in North Lawndale,''
says photographer Bruce
Talamon. ''I tried very hard to
find them, but it was tough.''
Photographer:
Bruce Talamon, USA

● *Above*

May 2nd was a big day for the
Morgan family of Harlow, Eng-
land. They were headed for a
Hawaiian vacation aboard United
Airlines Flight 1 out of Chicago.

Photographer Douglas Kirkland
also had a big day. His assignment was to shoot America's
first sunrise over Maine's Mount
Katahdin (see page 1) and sunset
the same day over Maui. He was
halfway to Hawaii when he made
this picture.
Photographer:
Douglas Kirkland, Canada

● *Left*

Josephine Mendez, 60, still works as a migrant farm worker, but thanks to her long years of toil, her son Edward Agundez does not have to anymore. A graduate of California State Polytechnic University, Agundez runs personnel management programs for area farmers.
Photographer:
Mario Pignata-Monti, Argentina

● *Following page*

Most *Day in the Life of America* photographers ran themselves ragged on May 2nd covering dozens of different people and situations. Belgian photographer John Vink had a simpler, but perhaps more challenging assignment: He spent the entire day riding the rails in an empty boxcar between Denver, Colorado, and Spokane, Washington, with Gypsy, a self-described hobo born in Wyoming.
Photographer:
John Vink, Belgium

Photographs by John Vink

● *Above*

Alexander Joseph, 49, a self-avowed polygamist and former fundamentalist Mormon, lives with nine of his ten "wives," eight sons and seven of his nine daughters on Long Haul Estate near Big Water, Utah. Joseph is pictured here with "wives" Joanna, Pamela, Boudicca, Diane, Delinda, Elizabeth, Dawn and Leslie. According to Boudicca (first row, second from the right), "This lifestyle is just the ticket for a woman of the '80s. Since we share all the cooking and housework, it's ideal for a woman who wants a career and a family."
Photographer:
Michele Cardon, USA

● *Right*

The Reverend Jim Bakker and his gospel-singing wife, Tammy, are the founders and stars of the PTL ("Praise the Lord" or "People That Love") Christian television network, which claims over ten million daily viewers around the world. At Heritage, USA, their combination headquarters and 2,500-acre evangelical resort in Ft. Mill, South Carolina, the indoor Main Street features a vaulted, sky-blue ceiling and drifting artificial clouds. Aside from her regular evangelical duties, Tammy has written two books (*Run to the Roar* and *Got to Be Me*) and has lent her name to a line of cosmetics.
Photographer:
Jerry Valente, USA

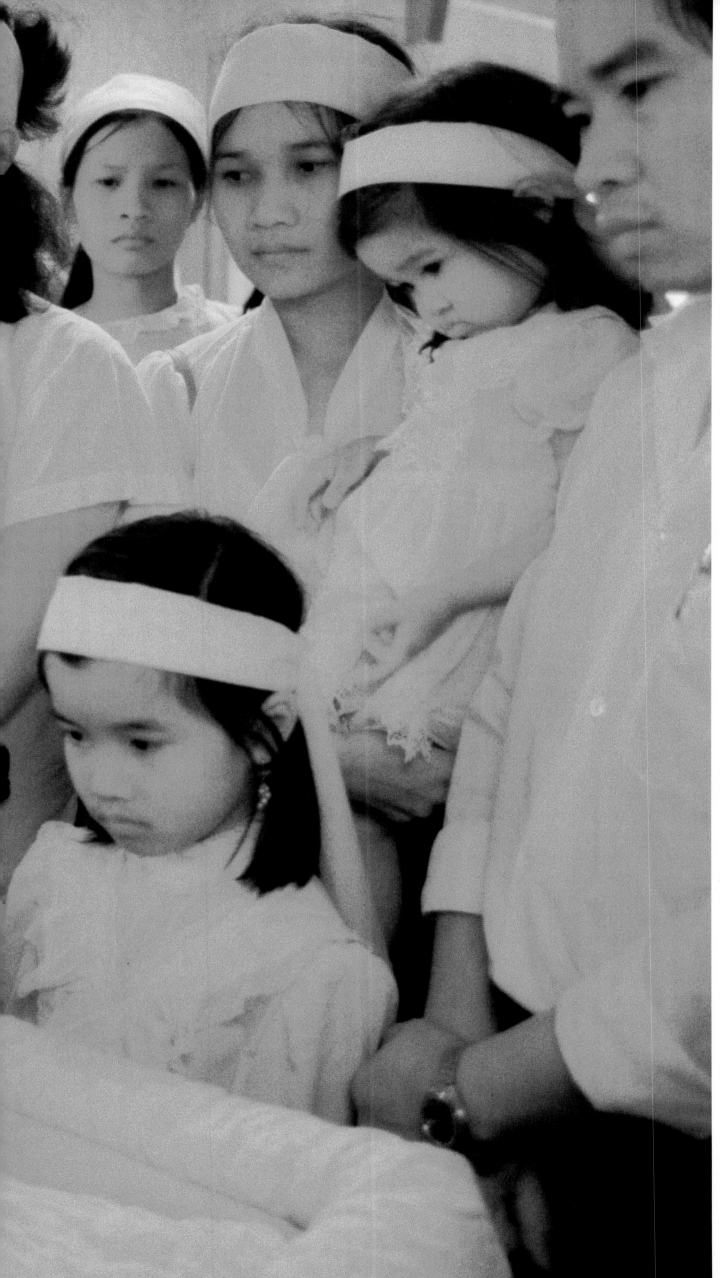

Twenty-year-old Thai Van Nguyen died on Monday, April 28, when a wall collapsed at an old house he was demolishing in Bay St. Louis, Mississippi. On May 2nd, his family, wearing the traditional white of Vietnamese mourning, gathered for a wake at nearby Edmond Fahey Funeral Home. Nguyen was buried in a Roman Catholic ceremony the following day, two years after he arrived in the United States from Vietnam.

Photographer Alain Keler says, ''The Vietnamese in Mississippi are a very traditional people. They teach their children to speak Vietnamese. They cook Vietnamese food. The whole family—from Biloxi and even other areas along the coast—sends money to buy materials for a fishing boat. They try not to have much to do with other Americans, but on the other hand, they have television, which is a strong influence on the children and young people. Slowly, television will assimilate the Vietnamese fishermen into American society.''

Photographer:
Alain Keler, France

123

Drama students from the North Carolina School of the Arts attend Jared Sakren's mask class at the Mount Pleasant Methodist Church in Winston-Salem, North Carolina.

Part of the University of North Carolina, North Carolina School of the Arts offers instruction in drama, dance, music, design and production to 750 students at all levels from high school to graduate school. Alumni include several well-known stage and screen actors (Terrence Mann, Tom Hulce), as well as opera singers (John Cheek of the Met), dancers (Mel Tomlinson) and internationally known classical musicians (such as flutist Ransom Wilson).

Photographer:
Claus C. Meyer, Brazil

● *Above*

After a 66-year professional
career, actress Helen Hayes
retired from live performance in
1971. But on May 2nd, the first
lady of American theater took
the stage and fielded questions
from drama students at the North
Carolina School of the Arts in
Winston-Salem.
Photographer:
Claus C. Meyer, Brazil

● *Right*

Outside a nearby rehearsal hall,
limber School of the Arts students warm up for dance class.
Photographer:
Claus C. Meyer, Brazil

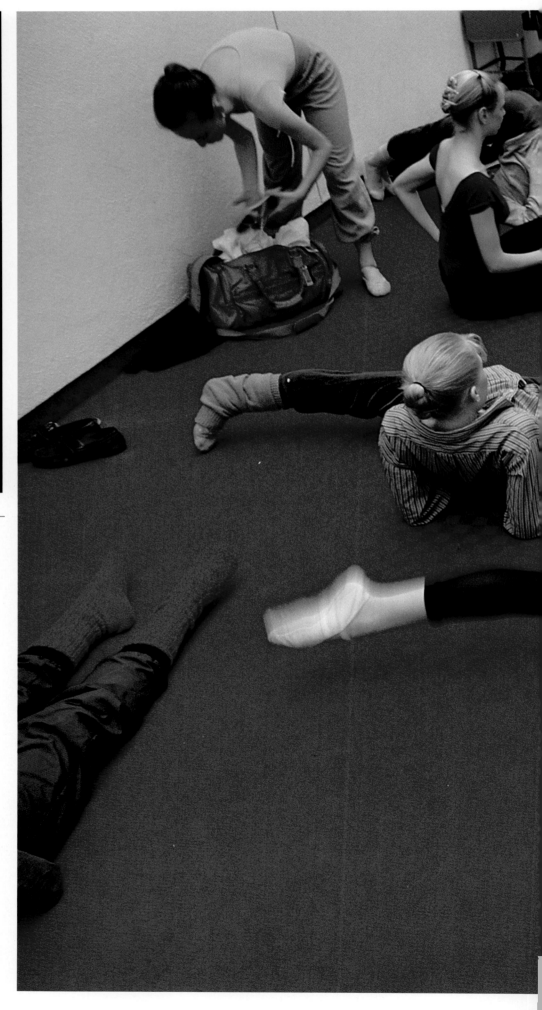

Barry Lewis

• *Previous page*

Bill Angers is one of three window-washers who spend all of their working hours improving the view from the Hyatt Regency Hotel in downtown Dallas, Texas. Reflected in the windows is the site of the Texas Book Depository, where Lee Harvey Oswald fired the fatal shots that killed President John F. Kennedy in 1963.

Photographer:

Barry Lewis, Britain

• *Above*

Window cleaner Danny Thomas and financial branch manager Robert Leacox at work on the 39th floor of Denver's 56-story Republic Plaza. Completed in 1984, Colorado's tallest building boasts 1,200,000 square feet of office space and 55,000 square feet of shops.

Photographer:

Alan Berner, USA

• *Right*

Aerobics are the lunch-time fare on the roof of the downtown International Athletic Club in health-conscious Denver, Colorado.

Photographer:

Alan Berner, USA

First graders Stephanie Bar-
rowman and Meghan Courtney
share a secret outside Apollo
Elementary School in Titusville,
Florida. The school opened 19
years ago when the Apollo Lunar
Program was operating full tilt at
nearby Kennedy Space Center.
Roughly half the school's students have at least one parent
who works for NASA or related
private companies.
Photographer:
Penny Tweedie, Britain

Children see the world with fresh eyes. On Friday, May 2nd, Kodak supplied two hundred American school children with Kodak Disc Cameras. In return for working on *A Day in the Life of America*, the children were allowed to keep their cameras. On this page is a selection from the 9,600 photographs shot by this army of young photographers.

Dennis Towne, Age 13   **Manti, Utah**

Misty Colvin, Age 12   **Riggins, Idaho**

Nettie Ann Alvarez, Age 10   **Denver, Colorado**

Brian McAdam, Age 8   **Littleton, Colorado**

Misty Colvin, Age 12   **Riggins, Idaho**

Douglas Kacena, Age 10   **Littleton, Colorado**

Gwyneth Campbell, Age 13   Lakewood, Colorado

Theo Bush, Age 7   Denver, Colorado

Sarah Cook, Age 9   Englewood, Colorado

Bevin Carithers, Age 12   Arvada, Colorado

Jason Scott Smith, Age 10   Jeffersonville, Indiana

Sky Patterson, Age 8   San Antonio, Texas

● *Above, top*

A photo-collage by graduating senior Alexander Frankfurter attracts attention at the Rhode Island School of Design's Woods-Gerry Gallery in Providence.
Photographer:
Gianfranco Gorgoni, Italy

● *Above*

On the set of his latest film at Astoria Studios in Queens, New York, director Woody Allen lines up a shot with cinematographer Carlo DiPalma.
Photographer:
Steve McCurry, USA

● *Below*

"Linda," a 1983 work by hometown sculptor John DeAndrea, is
one of the big draws at the
Denver Art Museum. The stun-
ningly lifelike effect was achieved
by making a vinyl mold of model
Linda Keller.
Photographer:
Alan Berner, USA

● *Following page*

The weekly baptism ceremony
at the Heritage Grand Hotel in
Fort Mill, South Carolina. The
hotel is a part of Heritage, USA,
a Christian community headed
by television evangelists Jim and
Tammy Bakker.
Photographer:
Jerry Valente, USA

● *Above*

Mary Kay Ash is, without doubt, the world's number one dispenser of pink Cadillacs. As of May 1986, she had given away 459 as bonuses to her superstar salespeople. Mary Kay's marketing team consists of 100,000 women, mostly part-timers, who sell her moderately priced cosmetics to friends and neighbors in living rooms across America. Mary Kay Cosmetics, Inc., founded on a shoestring in 1963, is privately owned (principally by Mary Kay herself) and therefore not required to state its profits publicly. But it can be safely said that Mary Kay—seen here with her poodle Gigi outside their Dallas home—is one Texan not terribly worried about 1986's falling oil prices.

Photographer:
Barry Lewis, Britain

● *Right*

Donnell Smith, 22, is an aspiring drummer and bassist who lives in Manhattan's trendy East Village. ''I always try to dress up,'' he says. ''It's important to have the proper attire.''

Photographer:
Raphaël Gaillarde, France

● *Left*

A basic wash, cut and dry costs $40 at Carlo Manfredi's Hair-power on Manhattan's St. Mark's Place. Hairpower is open from 10 a.m. to midnight seven days a week. Like many East Village shopowners, Manfredi is being forced out after 16 years by a fivefold rent increase—to $10,000 a month for his 500-square-foot shop.
Photographer:
Steve McCurry, USA

● *Above*

Housewife Edna Lautenschlager under the dryer at Georgetta's Styling Salon in Palmer, Nebraska (population: 450). Owner Georgetta Platt charges $10 for a wash, cut and dry.
Photographer:
Maddy Miller, USA

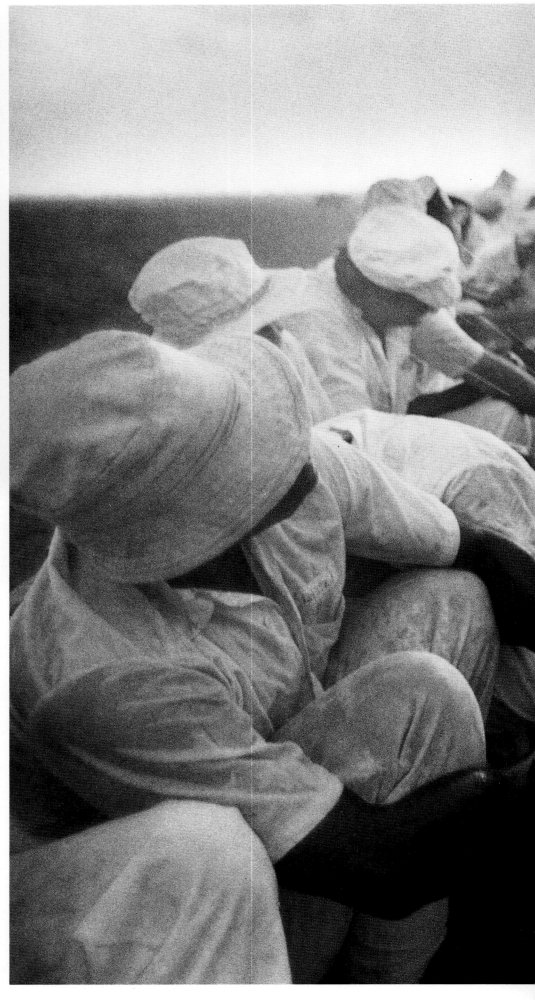

● *Above*

In January 1984, Martin Carrillo, 30, joined the more than 2,700 convicts doing time in the Texas state prison system for a drug offense (in his case, possession of heroin, in El Paso). Carrillo's maximum sentence of six years is just over half the state-wide average for new inmates.
Photographer:
Ethan Hoffman, USA

● *Right*

Ramsey Units I, II and III of the Texas Department of Corrections house more than 3,500 inmates—nearly a tenth of the state's total prison population—on an 18,000-acre farm near Angleton, Texas. Squads of 25 to 30 prisoners work eight hours a day, five days a week at Ramsey's agricultural operation. On May 2nd, this group waited in a driving rainstorm for more than an hour while guards chased down—and eventually caught—a prisoner who tried to escape.
Photographer:
Ethan Hoffman, USA

Life is just a fantasy for Siegfried & Roy, the German-born ''master illusionists'' whose stage spectacular, *Beyond Belief*, has been headlining at Las Vegas' Frontier Hotel since 1981. On May 2nd, *Day in the Life of America* photographer Francois Robert visited ''the Wizards of Joy'' at their nearby $10 million home, ''Jungle Palace,'' where the attractions included two rare white tigers (white with black stripes), an even rarer snow white tiger (completely white with ice blue eyes), and a fancy bit of levitation.

Robert (pronounced *row-bear*) says, ''After a long negotiation with their manager, we arrived at Siegfried & Roy's well-protected mansion and were admitted along with a local television news crew. I wanted to shoot the levitation over water, and, being master showmen, they agreed to do it in the tiger pen. As we discussed earlier, I set up my cameras and then left the scene. When they called us back 25 minutes later, Roy was already levitating. I never found out how they did it, but in a way, I'm glad. I'd rather believe there's still some magic in the world.''

Photographer:
**Francois Robert,
Switzerland**

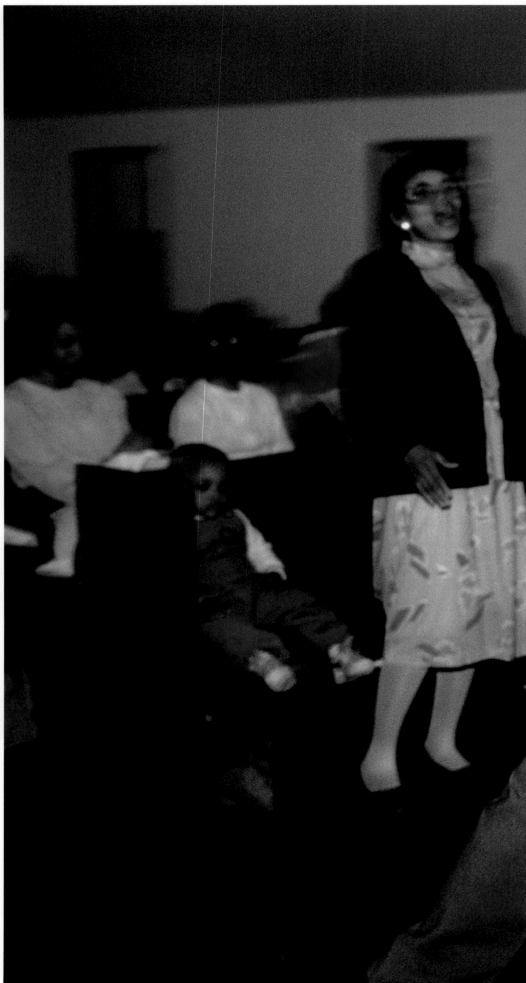

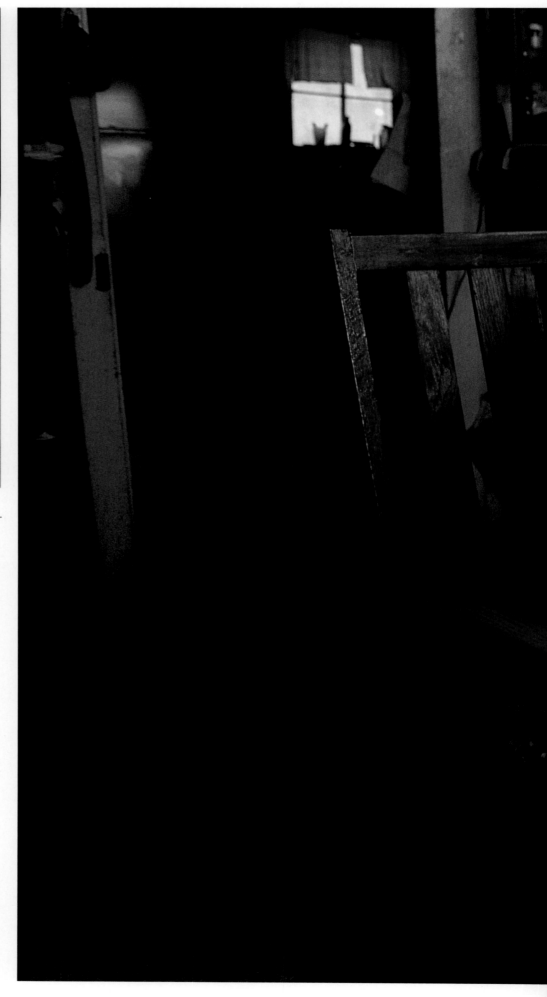

● *Above*

Frank and Margery Brown of Chelsea, Vermont, are members of the Ed Larkin Contra Dancers. On May 2nd, they showed their stuff in Chelsea Town Hall. Contra dancing is a type of square dancing, done in lines instead of squares. The 40-member group—named for fiddle player Ed Larkin who started the group in 1934—has about 40 regular members with an average age of 69.

Photographer:

Christopher Pillitz, Britain

● *Right*

B. T. (''Bennie'') Wrinkle, 85, cares full-time for his wife, Minnie, confined by strokes and heart trouble to a hospital bed in their living room. Wrinkle still grows vegetables and churns his own butter on a farm his grandfather started a century ago in Lebanon, Missouri.

Photographer:

Patrick Tehan, USA

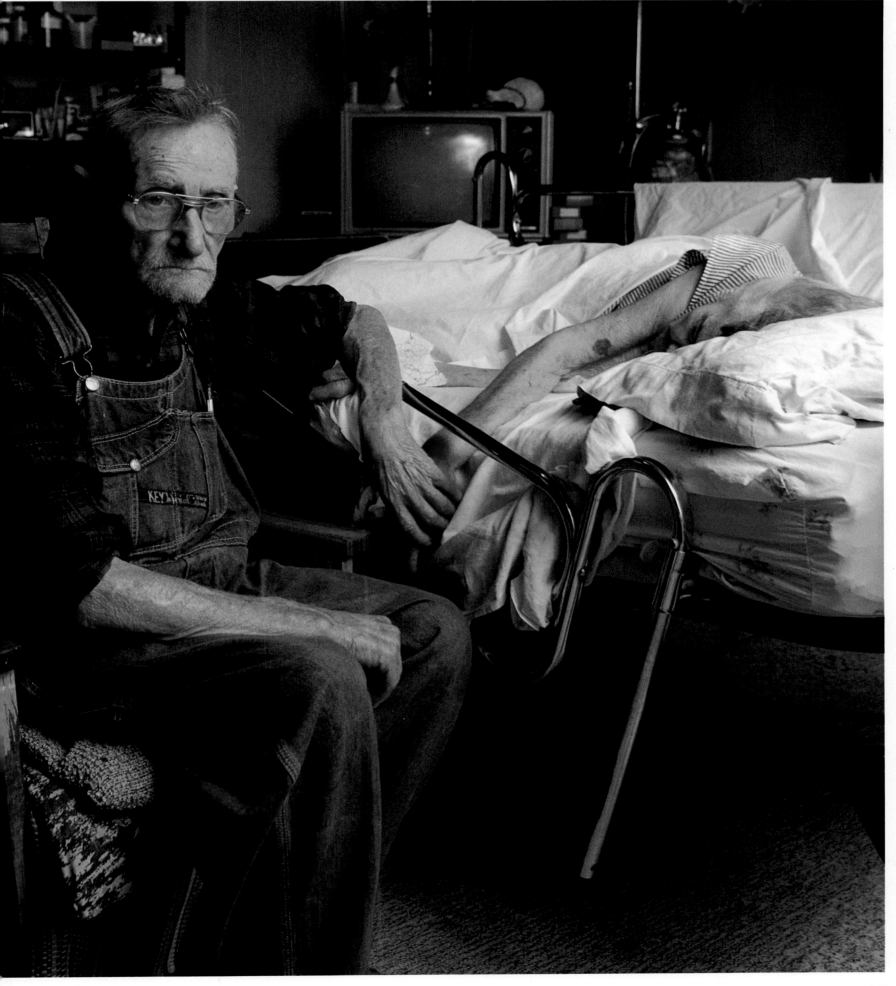

● *Left*

She used to bring a hymnal, but now this true believer brings her ''box'' to record a live gospel music performance outside Reverend Tim Hicks' trailer church in Soperton, Georgia.
Photographer:
Tomasz Tomaszewski, Poland

● *Above*

They used to call it recess, but in 1986, it's ''physical development time'' for 130 kids age two through six at the Palo Alto Preschool Center in Glendale, Arizona.
Photographer:
Andy Hernandez, Philippines

● *Following page*

Big bucks: Elaina Britton, 5, comes face to face with Alexander Hamilton of ten-dollar-bill fame at the Great American Marketplace exhibit in Oklahoma City's Enterprise Square.
Photographer:
Daniel Aubry, USA

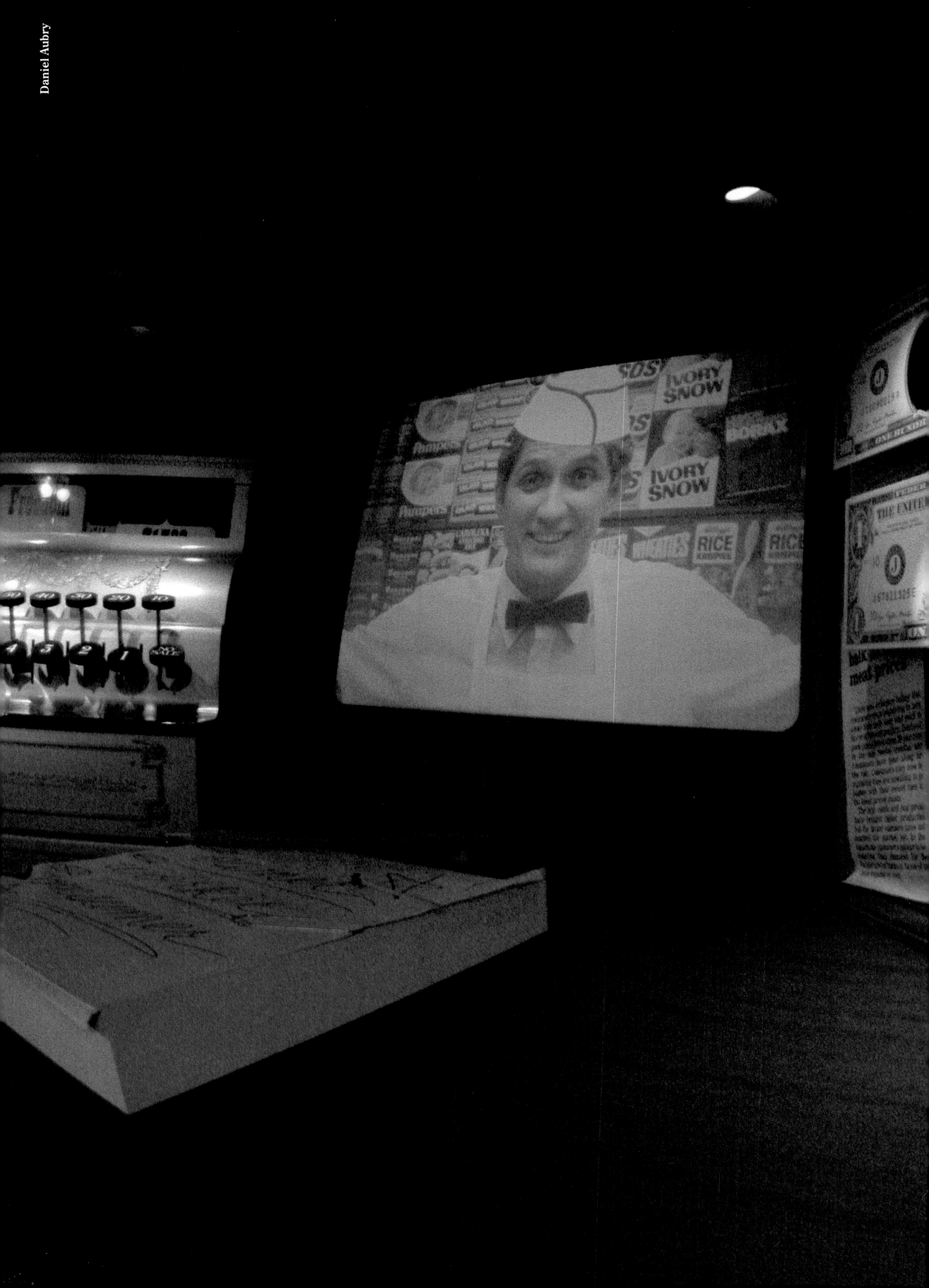

Daniel Aubry

A special seminar has been announced for grocery store owners to consider new ways to increase sales. The sessions will be conducted by Lee Warren Boswell who has spent many years in the food business.

The meetings will be held in the Civic Center at Lakeland, Florida, on September 8 and 9 starting at 9 a.m.

Those interested in attending the meetings should write the Florida Grocery Association, 309 North Iowa Ave., Lakeland, Florida, for more information.

● *Above*

Textile workers head home after
the early shift (7 a.m. to 3 p.m.)
at the Fieldcrest Cannon sheet
and towel mill in Kannapolis,
North Carolina.

Photographer:

Peter Turnley, USA

● *Right*

Clerk Matthew Barrall contem-
plates the ruins of a rough day in
the trading pits at the Chicago
Options Exchange where a total
of 438,000 contracts changed
hands on May 2nd.

Photographer:

Paul Chesley, USA

● *Following pages 160-161*
Lizzy Mack, 12, lives with her mother, brother and sister in a single room on Manhattan's West Side. The room is paid for by New York's Emergency Assistance for Families program. Photographer Letizia Battaglia says, "Lizzy is like a First Lady, a star of society. She is intelligent, good and beautiful—but she is poor. That is the only difference."

Photographer:

Letizia Battaglia, Italy

● *Following pages 162-163*
The first Friday in May is International Tuba Day in Harrisburg, Pennsylvania. Joel Day, coordinator of the event, says, "If you don't play the tuba, International Tuba Day is your day to recognize tuba players as talented masters of musical performance. If you do play, it's your day to relax and enjoy your much deserved recognition."

Photographer:

Volker Hinz, West Germany

● *Left and above*

In December 1982, the U.S. Environmental Protection Agency declared the town of Times Beach, Missouri, a hazardous area due to contamination by dioxin, a suspected carcinogen that had been added to the town's road-paving mixture. Of the 2,042 former residents, only George and Lorene Klein still remain. The Kleins risk dioxin poisoning because they are unwilling to settle for the $26,800 which the government is offering as compensation for their house. They insist it is worth more than twice that amount.

Photographer:

Stormi Greener, USA

Letizia Battaglia

New Ulm, Minnesota　　　　　　　　　　　　　　　　　　　**Flip Schulke**

Gainesville, Georgia　　　　　　　　　　　　　　　　　　　**Gerrit Fokkema**

Eugene, Oregon　　　　　　　　　　　　　　　　　　　**Gianni Giansanti**

Reno, Nevada   Dana Fineman

Savannah, Georgia   Gerd Ludwig

Baltimore, Maryland   Luc Choquer

● *Previous page*

Amy Foote and Paul Neis are regular exercise partners at the Monday, Wednesday and Friday aerobics class at the San Mateo Nautilus Fitness Center in Albuquerque, New Mexico.

Photographer:
Arthur Grace, USA

● *Right*

Giovanni Rigato, his wife, Mary, and their daughters Bridget, 9 (center), and Elena, 10, in front of their row house on Albemare Street in the "Little Italy" section of East Baltimore. (Sister-in-law Bernadette Quinn and her two-year-old daughter Maria are on the steps.)

Rigato came to the United States from Bolzano in 1970 and now owns Capriccio Restaurant, around the corner on Fawn Street. The girls are wearing uniforms from nearby St. Stanislaus School. "Little Italy," a 12-block area near Baltimore's Inner Harbor, is one of the city's 237 identifiable neighborhoods.

Photographer:
Luc Choquer, France

● *Previous page*

Mrs. Robert Stott is a sponsor of the prestigious Delta Debutante Club. On May 2nd, she held afternoon tea lessons on the veranda of the Retzer home in Greenville, Mississippi. The young ladies on the left are "pages," age 12 and 13, who attend the debutantes at balls and dream of the day when they, too, will turn 18. The younger ladies to the right, age eight to ten, are called "little friends."

Photographer:

D. Gorton, USA

● *Left*

New York City real estate czar Donald Trump planted 21 eleven-foot Bradford pear trees on the terraces of his gilded Fifth Avenue showcase, Trump Tower.

Photographer:

Jodi Cobb, USA

● *Above*

Lt. Mark J. Kerski applies an official "bust" sticker to the 110-foot U.S. Coast Guard vessel *Sea Hawk* in its home port of Key West, Florida. Each leaf symbol represents a marijuana seizure, and each snowflake, a cocaine seizure. Between 1972 and May 1986, the U.S. Coast Guard intercepted over 25 million pounds of marijuana and 10,000 pounds of cocaine—probably a small fraction of the illegal drugs that entered the United States during that period.

Photographer:

Robb Kendrick, USA

Melvin Red Cloud, great-grandson of the famous Sioux chief, paints grave markers in the carpenter's shop at Pine Ridge's Holy Rosary Mission, run by the Jesuits. The crosses will mark previously unmarked graves at the Oglala town cemetery.

Don Doll is chairman of the visual and performing arts department at Creighton University, an active photojournalist and a Jesuit priest. For the past ten years, he has documented the life and times of the Sioux Indians on South Dakota reservations. On May 2nd, Doll returned to South Dakota to photograph a day in the life of the Pine Ridge Reservation.

Photographer Doll says, "When I saw Melvin, I was reminded of all the friends I have lost to alcoholism, violence and suicide."

Photographer:
Don Doll, S.J., USA

● *Above, top*

Robin Thunder Horse, 20, and Charles Alcott, 17, at home with their two-week-old son, Corey. Alcott, who is half Navajo and half Sioux, is a junior at Red Cloud High School. Thunder Horse stays home with Corey. In the background is housemate Marlette Yellow Horse with her children.

Photographer:
Don Doll, S.J., USA

● *Above*

Robert Fast Horse, chief tribal judge, in his chambers at the tribal courthouse in Pine Ridge, South Dakota. Fast Horse, a graduate of the University of New Mexico School of Law, makes his rulings in accordance with the Oglala Sioux Tribe Law and Order Code, drafted by the tribal council.

Photographer:
Don Doll, S.J., USA

At the Vietnam War Memorial in Washington, D.C., Vietnam veteran Gary Wright Jr. of McLean, Virginia, gives his son Gary III a boost to kiss the name of his grandfather, Col. Gary G. Wright Sr., who is missing in action.
Photographer:
Seny Norasingh, Laos

Dave Shippee

● *Previous page*

Basque sheepherder Francisco
Lezamiz tends a band of approx-
imately 2,300 sheep in the hills
outside Emmett, Idaho.
Lezamiz, who works for the
Highland Livestock and Land
Company of Emmett, spends
nine months of the year camping
out with the animals. He came to
America from northern Spain in
1972 and is one of over 4,000
Basques who reside in Idaho—
many of whom work as
sheepherders.
Photography contest winner:
Dave Shippee, USA

● *Left*

On May 2nd, Americans were
preparing for the upcoming
Statue of Liberty Centennial
Celebration. Photographer Dilip
Mehta encountered the refur-
bished 225-ton, 152-foot-high
lady in a striking late afternoon
light.
Photographer:
Dilip Mehta, Canada

● *Above*

Marvin Williams (left) and
Marvin Stevens, maintenance
men, cleaning up at the
Paramus Park Shopping Center
in Paramus, New Jersey.
Photographer:
Diego Goldberg, Argentina

● *Left*

Airman First Class Mark Nowotny, a 26-year-old maintenance specialist, washes the canopy of a T-38A advanced jet trainer used by student test pilots at Edwards Air Force Base, home of "the right stuff."
Photographer:
Roger Ressmeyer, USA

● *Above*

The Space and Rocket Center of Hunstville, Alabama, operates the United States Space Camp, where children ages 10-15 spend a week learning the basics of space travel. Here, Tony Garner lends a helping hand to fellow camper Christian Conte.
Photographer:
Debra Schulke, USA

Hot young fashion photographer Sante D'Orazio was born and raised in Brooklyn. Model Kristen McMenamy grew up in Allentown, Pennsylvania, and began her professional career in New York in November 1984. On May 2nd, they worked together on a Manhattan rooftop shooting an ad for a European lingerie company.

Burk Uzzle, who photographed this rooftop scene, chose his shooting technique very carefully. He says, ''My assignment was to shoot the fashion industry backstage, the flip side of the slick fashion photographs that we all see on the cover of *Vogue*. I did all my shooting in black and white to separate my shots very quickly from ordinary fashion photos. I also decided to use a wide angle lens almost all the time in order to show these people in context and to give the viewer an idea of the extraordinary things the photographer and model go through to get glamorous pictures.''

Photographer:
Burk Uzzle, USA

The *Day in the Life* sponsors and *Popular Photography* magazine issued a challenge to photographers: "Dust off your cameras on May 2nd and match your photographic skills against 200 of the world's top photojournalists." A host of talented photographers accepted the challenge and entered their best efforts in the *Day in the Life of America* photography contest. Some of the entries are seen on this page. Others appear throughout the book.

Jockey's Ridge, Outer Banks, North Carolina   Henry Stindt

Braddock, Pennsylvania   Jack McKenzie

Cambridge, Massachusetts   Elizabeth Wilson

Maui, Hawaii   Sherry Lee Thompson

Washington, D.C.   William E. Woolam

Erie, Pennsylvania   Diane R. McCafferty

186

Houston, Texas   Rob Muir

New York, New York   Shaun Considine

New Vienna, Iowa   Julie Habel

Houston, Texas   Rob Muir

Pace, Mississippi   Jeff McAdory

Line Creek, Wyoming   Mark A. Payler

Florida "mermaids" suit up for an underwater extravaganza at Weeki Wachee Spring near Orlando.
Photographer:
Misha Erwitt, USA

Bob Montgomery, a Washington, D.C., law student, dives into the rooftop pool at the Eldorado Hotel in Santa Fe, New Mexico.
Photographer:
Arnaud de Wildenberg, France

A trainer takes time out for a trick with one of his charges at the Dolphin Research Lab in Marathon, Florida.
Photographer:
Jennifer Erwitt, USA

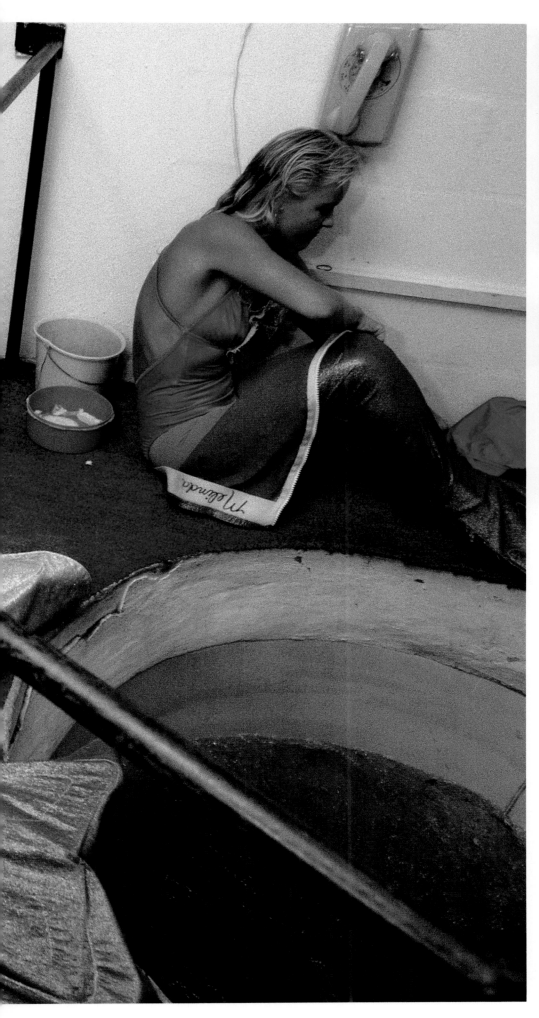

● Above and right

After-school dancing class at the Round Hill Community House is an adolescent rite of passage in affluent Greenwich, Connecticut. Parents of these fourth graders pay $95 for ten one-hour Friday afternoon sessions. Barclay Classes, of Westfield, New Jersey, runs similar programs for children age nine to fourteen in 21 other towns throughout the Northeast. According to director William Thomson, students learn all the traditional ballroom dances —including the waltz, fox-trot,

cha-cha and rumba—as well as "basic manners and social niceties."

On May 2nd, Kathy Shaio (in white lace and bow) went to dance class after her regular studies at Greenwich Country Day School. Kathy says that she likes the rumba best because "it's the most exciting."

Photographer:
Nicole Bengiveno, USA

Mayor George Ahmaogak Sr. presides over Alaska's North Slope Borough, an 80,000-square-mile expanse of ice and tundra that includes the town of Barrow, seven smaller villages and 20% of America's daily oil production. Ahmaogak—like 80% of his 8,300 constituents—is an Iñupiat Eskimo, one of Alaska's original inhabitants. Each spring, Ahmaogak heads out to hunt whales the old-fashioned way, through breaks in the Arctic Ocean ice pack.

All 200 *Day in the Life of America* photographers were asked to make a portrait of the mayor of the town or city where they were assigned. Photographer Jim Balog made this shot of Mayor Ahmaogak eight miles out on the ice pack off Barrow, Alaska. Other *Day in the Life* photographers worked in more temperate surroundings, photographing hizzoners ranging from New York's flamboyant Edward Koch to Cuba, Kansas' Steve Benyshek. Photographer D. Gorton, however, found the only mayor, male or female, who wanted to pose in ballet tights and a tutu, Greenville, Mississippi's William C. Burnley Jr. To meet a sampling of America's mayors, please turn the page.

Photographer:
James Balog, USA

America's Mayors

All 200 *Day in the Life of America* photographers
were asked to photograph the top municipal officials
in the city or town where they were assigned.

Steve Benyshek
Cuba, Kansas

Ace Barton
Riggins, Idaho

Andrew Young
Atlanta, Georgia

Tom Sawyer
Key West, Florida

Pawnee Bill Smith
Hooverville, Kansas

Tom Kough
Austin, Minnesota

Mary Anderson
Kinney, Minnesota

Sonny Scalese
Sunburst, Montana

Richard Nordvold
Hibbing, Minnesota

Robert Kozaren
Hamtramck, Michigan

Dennis Chamberlin

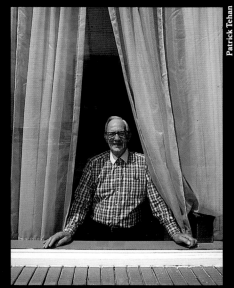

Howard Johnson
Buffalo, Missouri

Patrick Tehan

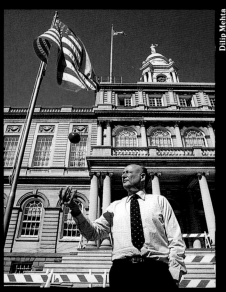

Edward Koch
New York City, New York

Dilip Mehta

Page Worth
Belfast, Maine

Graeme Outerbridge

Cesar Dabdoub Chavez and Marcelino Varona
Nogales Sonora, Mexico and Nogales, Arizona

Sara Krulwich

Kenneth Henke Jr.
Keokuk, Iowa

Andy Nelson

Frank Radford
Soperton, Georgia

Tomasz Tomaszewski

William C. Burnley Jr.
Greenville, Mississippi

D. Gorton

Dianne Feinstein
San Francisco, California

Yan Morvan

195

● *Left*

In Sacramento, California, Jerry McCarthy and Renee Jenkins warm up for an evening concert featuring country-rock band Alabama.

Photographer:
Susan Biddle, USA

● *Above*

Linda Scalese, 18, shows off her wedding dress to best friends Patricia Kimmet and Keri Alstad in her bedroom in Sunburst, Montana.

Photographer:
Yann Arthus-Bertrand, France

● *Right*

Paul Mello, a 23-year-old marine electrician, wanted his girlfriend's name inscribed on his shoulder in Chinese. On May 2nd, Buddy's Tattoo Shop in Newport, Rhode Island (''The Very Best in Tattooing, Since 1948. Individual Needles & Colours for Each Customer''), obliged. Buddy, who is also responsible for the dragon, got the proper Chinese characters—or at least a close approximation—from a waiter at a nearby Chinese restaurant.
Photographer:
Michael O'Brien, USA

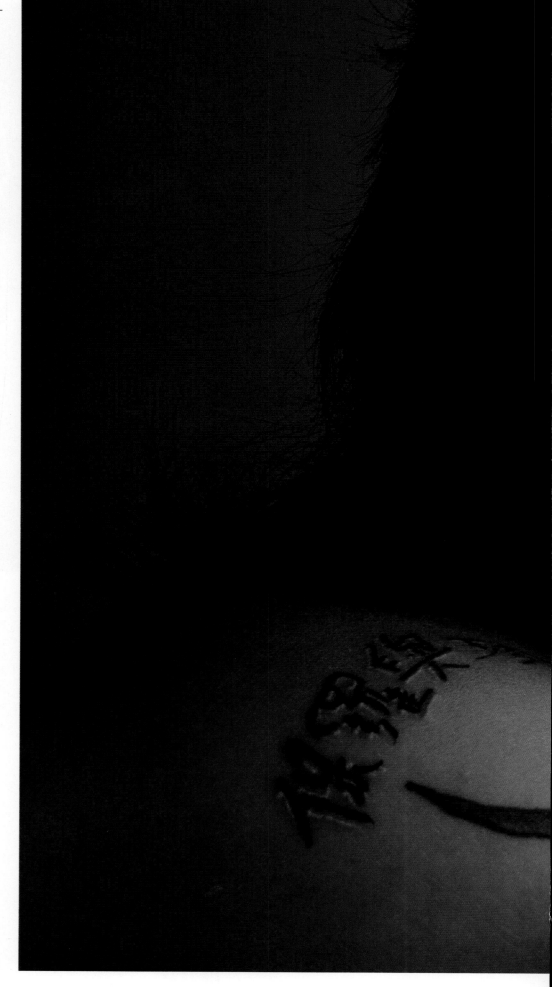

Two men assault a drunk in an alley off Winston Street in downtown Los Angeles, an area better known as "Skid Row." *Day in the Life of America* photographer Sarah Leen says, "I turned into an alley and saw a mugging down at the end of the block. My first instinct was, Can I change my lens fast enough? I stood there, and I photographed the whole incident, then the muggers started running up the alley toward me, and I quickly turned around so they couldn't see my cameras. But they just blew right by me and disappeared. I thought maybe I was shaking too much for the picture to come out."
Photographer:
Sarah Leen, USA

Savannah Highway, Charleston, South Carolina

Aaron Chang, USA

Highway 17, Charleston, South Carolina

Aaron Chang, USA

● *Previous page*

On Philadelphia's Schuylkill River, an eight-man shell ventures out of the University of Pennsylvania boathouse and into the early evening rower's rush hour.
Photographer:
Patrick Ward, Britain

● *Below*

Amy Treibick, 17, chats with her boyfriend, Scott, from her bedroom in Greenwich, Connecticut. Looking on is Kim Lopp, 16, a classmate at nearby Greenwich Academy.
Photographer:
Nicole Bengiveno, USA

● *Above, top*

At first, photographer David Turnley got a cold shoulder from these two young Puerto Rican girls on the street in New York City's ''Spanish'' (East) Harlem. ''But I told one of them that her perfume smelled nice, and all of a sudden, they went from being tough, street-hard people into little girls.''
Photographer:
David Turnley, USA

● *Above*

On May 2nd, 17-year-old Tiffany Stettner had a problem. She found out that her friend had just bought the same dress that she had planned to wear that night. ''At first it was traumatic,'' says Tiffany, who lives with her mother and stepfather in Miami's Quayside condominium complex, ''then when we faced reality, it just came down to which dress am I going to wear?'' (It turned out to be none of those pictured here.) A junior at Miami Country Day School and a former ''Little Miss Texas'' (at age 5), Tiffany says she wants to be a lawyer someday.
Photographer:
Lynn Goldsmith, USA

● *Previous page*

Girls' softball is serious business in Narragansett, Rhode Island. These 13- to 15-year-olds, sponsored by the Pit-N-Patio Pizza Parlor, wait in their Sprague Park dugout to bat against a squad backed by the Diso Corp.
Photographer:
Michael O'Brien, USA

● *Above*

On May 2nd, veteran Soviet photographer Yuri Abramochkin encountered a light rain on Highway 225 outside Houston, Texas.
Photographer:
Yuri Abramochkin, USSR

● *Right*

A Day in the Life of America photography contest winner Eric John Albrecht took this picture on state Route 651 near New Bedford in the heart of Ohio's Amish country. Albrecht, who works as a staff photographer for *The Columbus Dispatch*, says, "When I read about the contest, I knew I could take a picture good enough for the book. May 2nd was a beautiful day, and when I saw the light shining off the road and an Amish buggy drive by, I knew I had my shot."
Photography contest winner:
Eric John Albrecht, USA

● *Above*

Sitting on top of the world: Forrest Striegl, 80, is a retired county administrator from Wisconsin. Seven years ago he met Rose, his next door neighbor at the Top of the World retirement village in Clearwater, Florida. They were married a year later. Forrest was a lifelong bachelor before he met Rose, and his bride can't understand why. ''Forrest,'' she says, ''is just so terrific.''

Photographer:

Mary Ellen Mark, USA

● *Right*

On May 2nd, Robert Izumi and his 91-year-old great-grand-mother, Yei Harimoto, went to Honolulu's Ala Moana Park to watch the sun set over the Pacific. Izumi, 16, is a *rokusei*— one of a handful of sixth-genera-tion Japanese-Americans. He can trace his ancestry back to Goha-chiro Namura, a *samurai* who served as chief interpreter for the first Japanese diplomatic mis-sion to the United States in 1860.

Photographer:

Eikoh Hosoe, Japan

● *Left*

At Chicago's South Shore Country Club, Mayor Harold Washington (at right, gray hair) greets Alderman Bobby Rush during a 55th-birthday dinner for construction company president C. F. Moore (far right). Washington, a former Democratic congressman, defeated incumbent Jane Byrne to become Chicago's first black mayor in 1983.

Photographer:

Francoise Huguier, France

● *Above*

An abandoned barbershop serves as an impromptu men's club on the corner of 19th and Market streets in East St. Louis, Illinois.

Photographer:

Eli Reed, USA

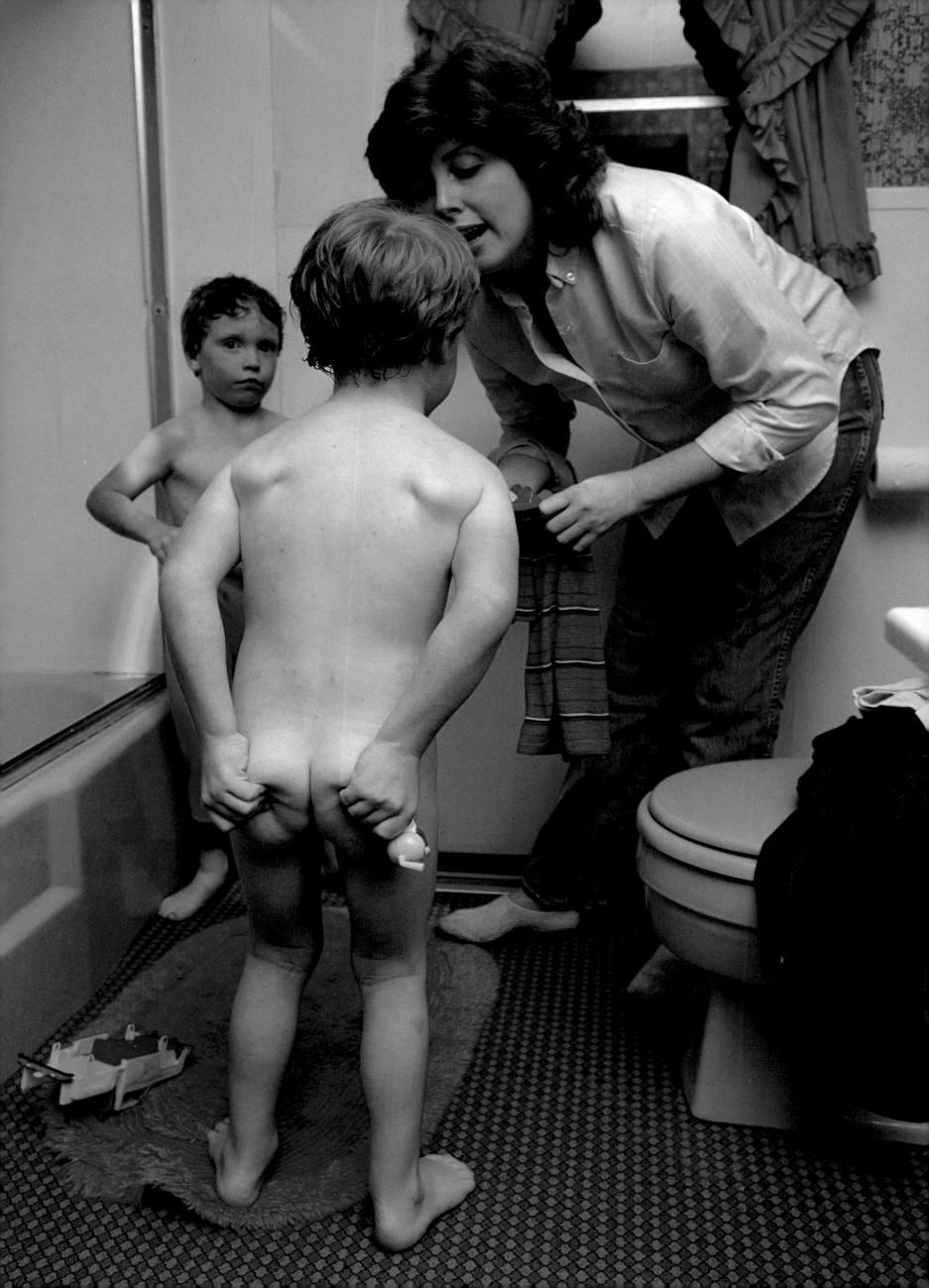

● *Left*

Linda Whaley consults her four-year-old identical twins, Jason and Jonathan, after a bath at their home in Sevierville, Tennessee.
Photographer:
Daniele Pellegrini, Italy

● *Above*

Budding belles at the Pink Marble Mansion, a country outpost of the Atlanta-based traveling finishing school, L'Ecole des Ingenues. Founded in 1976 by former model and fashion executive Anne Oliver, L'Ecole dishes up instruction in ''personal beauty, visual poise, fashion finesse, self-confidence, aesthetic awareness, etiquette and the social graces'' to young ladies age 11 to 28. Aside from the ten-day summer ''Finishing Camps'' at the mansion in the Blue Ridge Mountains north of Atlanta—priced at $2,000 per *ingenue*—Mrs. Oliver conducts weekend classes at the city's Ritz-Carlton Hotel (*Le Petit Programme*, $500) and $4,000 spring ''Finishing Tours'' to Europe.
Photographer:
P. F. Bentley, USA

● *Left and above*

Despite a judge's orders, the Ku Klux Klan in Hall County, Georgia, has taken to marching on mostly black sections of town in full regalia—ostensibly to protest the sale of drugs. Most folks around the county are embarrassed about the Klan's recent resurgence. Gainesville City Manager Ray Keith says succinctly, "We don't appreciate or need this type of activity in our city."

Retired poultry inspector Elizabeth Carey, seen at left with her 16-month-old great-granddaughter, Brandy Rowden, says she joined the Klan to fight "drug addiction and abortion clinics." But the big and rather more ominous draw still seems to be old-fashioned cross-burnings, like this one on May 2nd in an Oakwood Klansman's backyard.

Photographer:
Gerrit Fokkema, Australia

● *Right*

On May 2, 1986, America was worried about atomic fallout from the April 26th meltdown at the Chernobyl nuclear reactor in the Soviet Union. Meanwhile, at least part of the Three Mile Island nuclear power plant—site of America's own worst nuclear malfunction in 1979—was once again operating full steam ahead.

Three Mile Island's Unit 1 was reopened in October 1985, within 24 hours of a United States Supreme Court decision permitting its operation. To the left of its twin cooling towers stands ill-fated TMI Unit 2, where the partial meltdown occurred. Seven years after the Three Mile Island accident, workers were still cleaning up the radioactive mess in Unit 2, while Unit 1 was turning six pounds of enriched uranium a day into enough electricity to power 500,000 homes in eastern Pennsylvania and New Jersey.

Photographer:
Volker Hinz, West Germany

Since 1943 Richland, Washington, has been the proud home of Hanford Federal Nuclear Reservation, which boasts three operating reactors (including one that produces plutonium for warheads), a uranium reprocessing plant and tons of accumulated atomic waste. On May 2nd, Richland was continuing its three decade love affair with splitting atoms. Richland High School cheerleaders ("Home of the Bombers") were polishing up their favorite chant, "Bomber Power!!" And elsewhere around town, there was little doubt about how most local people—16,500 of whom work at the Hanford facility—feel about living with nukes. Said one local doctor: "The greatest hazard here is cigarette smoking."

Photographer:
Doug Menuez, USA

● *Above*

Prom night at the Linwood Country Club, New Jersey: 326 graduating seniors from Atlantic City High School paid $40 per couple to attend the gala event. The theme of the 1986 dance was ''The Best of Times.''
Photographer:
R. Ian Lloyd, Canada

Photographer Mary Ellen Mark shot 70 rolls of film on May 2nd, 11 in color and 59 black and white. Reproduced below is one of her contact sheets—(all of the images are from one roll of film)—showing the Gibbs Senior High School prom in St. Petersburg, Florida. Which photograph would you have selected for *A Day in the Life of America*? To see which frame the picture editors finally chose, please turn to the next page.

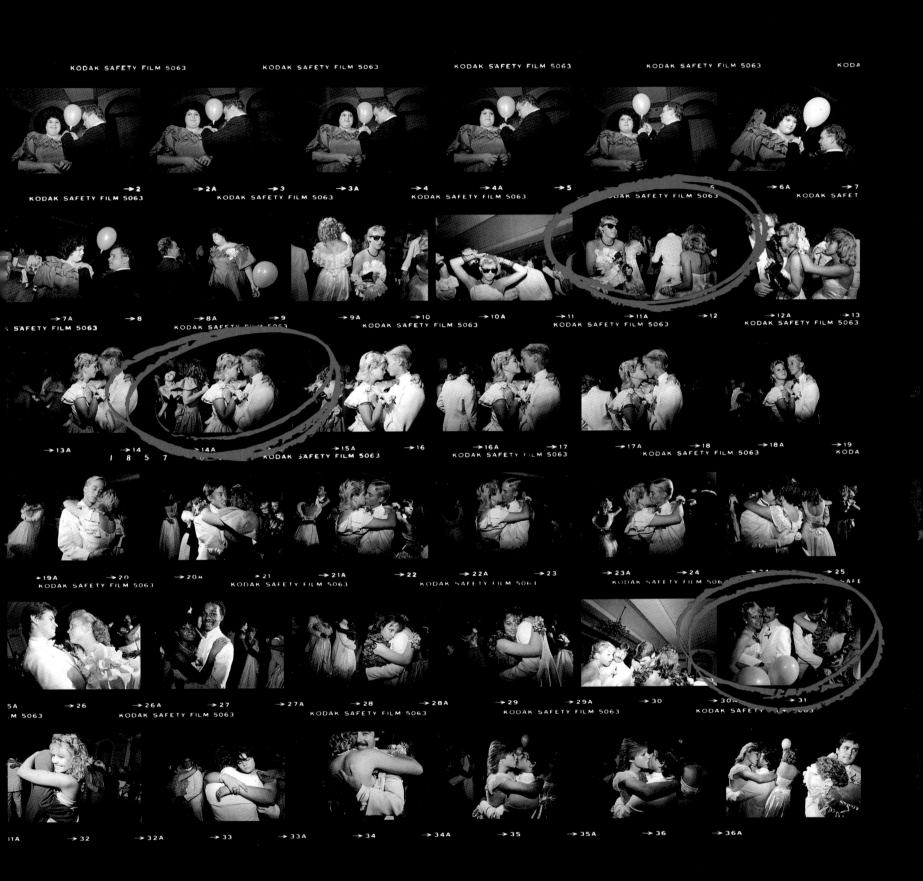

● *Previous page*

Although Mike Hunter is a feedlot cowboy, he and his wife, Carol, buy their meat wrapped in plastic like everyone else. On May 2nd, the Hunters brought daughters Kylee and Kalajo on a late-night shopping expedition to Dillon's Supermarket in Garden City, Kansas.
Photographer:
Chris Johns, USA

● *Above*

In the dressing room at Les Violins Supper Club on Miami's Biscayne Boulevard, showgirls Angela Lopez and Melanie Gilbert relax before a performance of "Grand Cabaret," a tribute to the great nightclub shows of the past. On May 2nd, the club was just about filled to its 500-seat capacity.
Photographer:
Stephanie Maze, USA

● *Right*

On May 2nd, at NBC's Studio 1 in Burbank, California, comedienne Joan Rivers makes what is probably her final appearance as perennial "guest host" of the popular "Tonight Show." Four days later, Rivers surprised the television world—and "Tonight Show" star Johnny Carson—by announcing that she had signed a three-year, multimillion dollar contract to launch her own, competing late-night talk show. A

Rivers spokesman said that Carson—who helped launch her show-biz career in the 1960s—hung up abruptly when she called to explain.
Photographer:
David Hume Kennerly, USA

● *Left*

"Smokey's Greatest Shows" brings a dozen rides and other attractions to Millinocket, Maine, each year in early May, courtesy of the local Elks club. "I shot in the Arctic for *A Day in the Life of Canada*, and the conditions were similar shooting this picture," says photographer Sam Garcia. "It was 29 degrees with a 30-mile-an-hour wind, but the carnival went on anyway."
Photographer:
Sam Garcia, USA

● *Above, top*

Stuart Parker, 24, and Robin Ritchie, 26, watch one of 1986's comedy hits, "Down and Out in Beverly Hills," at the Gem Theater in Kannapolis, North Carolina—the only show in town and one of the country's few remaining $1 movie houses.
Photographer:
Peter Turnley, USA

● *Above*

At the Beer Barn Drive Thru at the corner of Park Lane and Greenville Avenue in Dallas, you can buy beer, wine and light snacks without ever leaving your car. On a good weekend, the Beer Barn moves upwards of 150 16-gallon kegs of beer. Budweiser is most popular, Coors Lite a strong second.
Photographer:
Barry Lewis, Britain

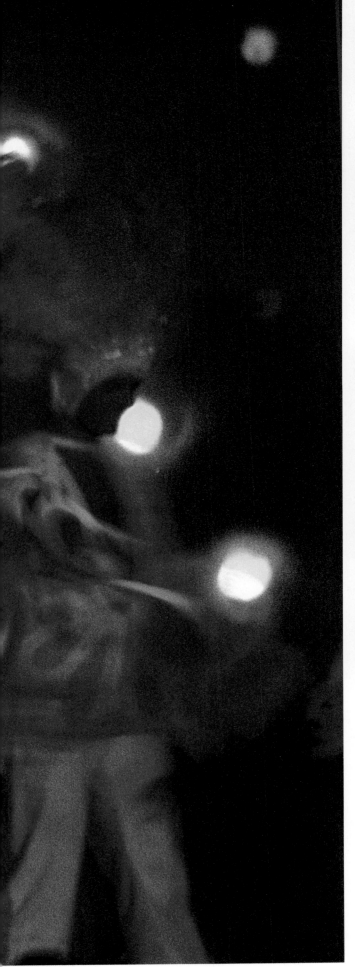

● *Left*

Maria Cabrera (left) and Maria Marrero join in a musical tribute to the old Tropicana nightclub in Havana, part of the nightly show ''Grand Cabaret'' at Les Violins Supper Club in Miami.

Photographer:

Stephanie Maze, USA

● *Above, top*

History as seen through the movies—from the 1906 San Francisco earthquake to the year 2001 (seen here)—is the theme of ''Hello Hollywood, Hello'' at Bally's Grand Hotel in Reno, Nevada. Produced on ''the world's largest stage'' at a cost said to top $5 million, the show wows 4200 wide-eyed newlyweds and jaded gamblers a night with 94 changes of scenery, 30,000 light bulbs and a cast of 100.

Photographer:

Dana Fineman, USA

● *Above*

Dancer Michaela Marshall, 20, arrived in Reno from Britain in 1985 to join the cast of ''Hello Hollywood, Hello.'' On May 2nd, photographer Dana Fineman caught her brushing her teeth between shows.

Photographer:

Dana Fineman, USA

● *Above*

Harlan Hubbard, an 86-year-old writer and artist, lives on what he calls "the fringe of society." He and his wife, Anna, 83, built their own finely crafted house—without telephone or electricity—on the banks of the Ohio River near Milton, Kentucky. For many years the Hubbards would play duets together in the evenings, Anna on the piano, Harlan on the violin, but on May 2nd, Harlan stayed up late reading and worrying about Anna, who was seriously ill in a nearby hospital.

Photographer:
Sara Grosvenor, USA

● *Right*

Manhattan's chic Palladium discotheque asked two *emigré* Soviet conceptual artists, Komar and Melamid, to satirically re-create May Day in Moscow's Red Square. The event (complete with a replica of Lenin's tomb and bartenders dressed as Soviet Boy Scouts) drew a capacity crowd of 4,400 late-night party-goers, at a very capitalist $15 a head.

Photographer:
Vladimir Sichov, Stateless

● *Following pages 246-247*

On May 2nd, L.W. Higgins High School in New Orleans held its prom—"A Night to Remember"—at the city's Royal Sonesta Hotel. Students who wanted to keep the night going longer found Bourbon Street's never-ending street party right outside the hotel doors.
Photographer:
David Alan Harvey, USA

● *Following pages 248-249*

Helicopter traffic-watchers call Chicago's busiest highway intersection "The Spaghetti Bowl." It's where the Dwight D. Eisenhower Expressway, the Dan Ryan Expressway and the John F. Kennedy Expressway all run together.
Photographer:
Paul Chesley, USA

● *Following pages 250-251*

As May 2nd draws to a close, a spring thunderstorm catches the Friday-night farm crowd drinking 65-cent beers at the Wagon Wheel Cafe in Cuba, Kansas.
Photographer:
Jim Richardson, USA

● *Left*

Ike and Mike's New Highland Inn in Bakersfield, California, furnishes the shirts and a $100 first prize for its weekly ''wet T-shirt'' contest. On May 2nd, bar patron Kenny Graham did the honors as sprayer for the 11 volunteer contestants. The winner was determined by cheers from the audience of 160.
Photographer:
Frank Fournier, France

● *Above*

''Hot Chocolate'' and ''Creme de Coco'' (they prefer to be known by their stage names) are singers at the Baby Grand Night Club on 125th Street in Harlem.
Photographer:
David Turnley, USA

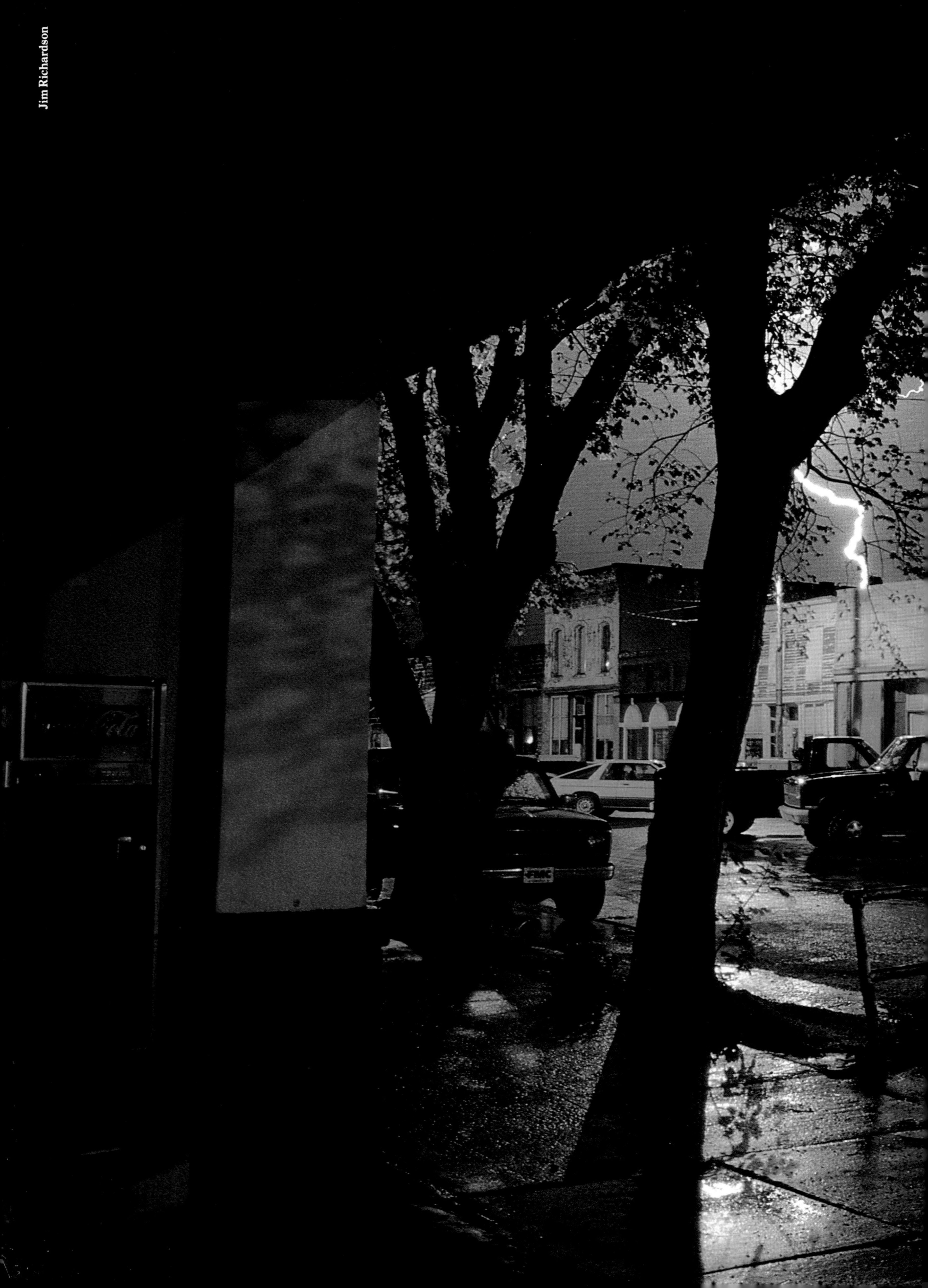

Jim Richardson

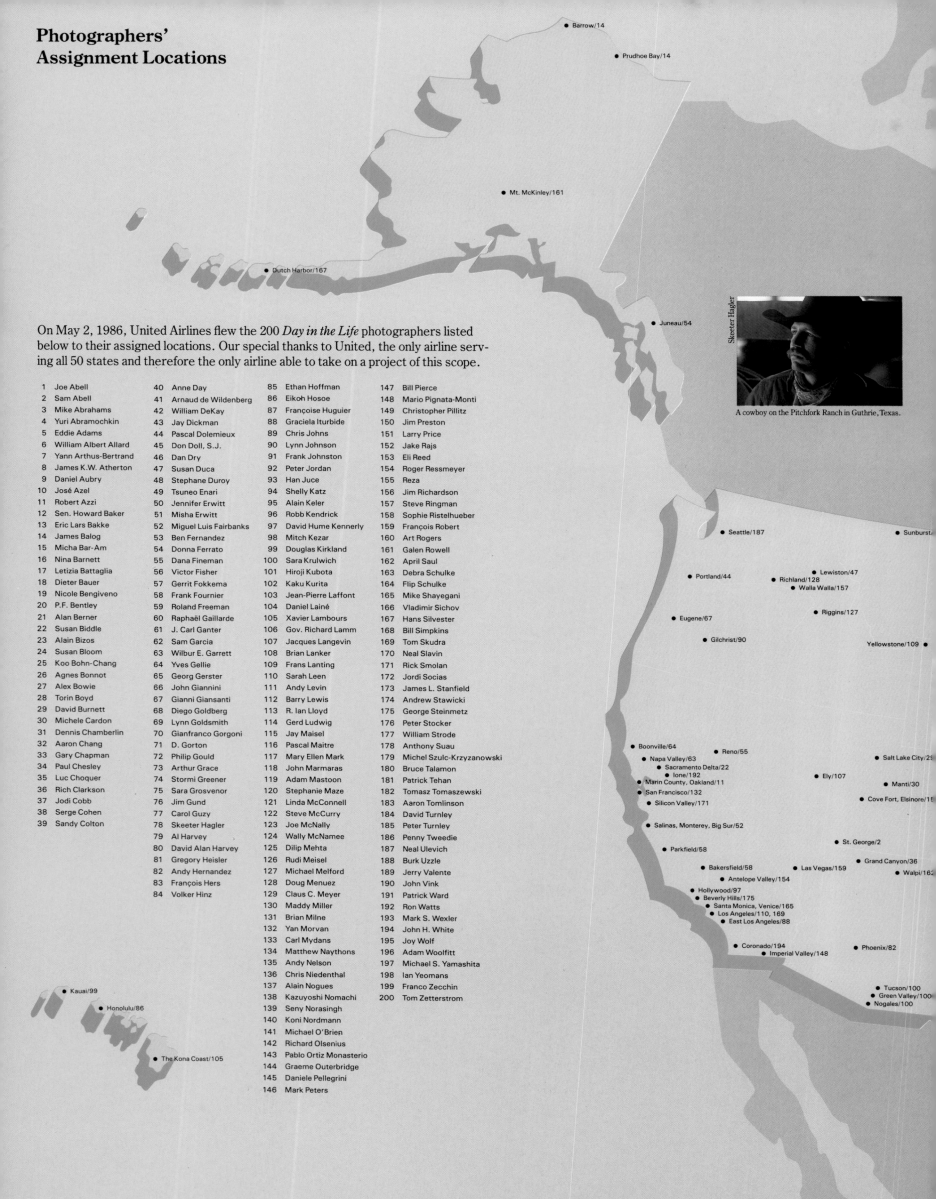

Photographers' Assignment Locations

Barrow/14

Prudhoe Bay/14

● Mt. McKinley/161

● Dutch Harbor/167

● Juneau/54

On May 2, 1986, United Airlines flew the 200 *Day in the Life* photographers listed below to their assigned locations. Our special thanks to United, the only airline serving all 50 states and therefore the only airline able to take on a project of this scope.

1 Joe Abell	40 Anne Day	85 Ethan Hoffman	147 Bill Pierce
2 Sam Abell	41 Arnaud de Wildenberg	86 Eikoh Hosoe	148 Mario Pignata-Monti
3 Mike Abrahams	42 William DeKay	87 Françoise Huguier	149 Christopher Pillitz
4 Yuri Abramochkin	43 Jay Dickman	88 Graciela Iturbide	150 Jim Preston
5 Eddie Adams	44 Pascal Dolemieux	89 Chris Johns	151 Larry Price
6 William Albert Allard	45 Don Doll, S.J.	90 Lynn Johnson	152 Jake Rajs
7 Yann Arthus-Bertrand	46 Dan Dry	91 Frank Johnston	153 Eli Reed
8 James K.W. Atherton	47 Susan Duca	92 Peter Jordan	154 Roger Ressmeyer
9 Daniel Aubry	48 Stephane Duroy	93 Han Juce	155 Reza
10 José Azel	49 Tsuneo Enari	94 Shelly Katz	156 Jim Richardson
11 Robert Azzi	50 Jennifer Erwitt	95 Alain Keler	157 Steve Ringman
12 Sen. Howard Baker	51 Misha Erwitt	96 Robb Kendrick	158 Sophie Ristelhueber
13 Eric Lars Bakke	52 Miguel Luis Fairbanks	97 David Hume Kennerly	159 François Robert
14 James Balog	53 Ben Fernandez	98 Mitch Kezar	160 Art Rogers
15 Micha Bar-Am	54 Donna Ferrato	99 Douglas Kirkland	161 Galen Rowell
16 Nina Barnett	55 Dana Fineman	100 Sara Krulwich	162 April Saul
17 Letizia Battaglia	56 Victor Fisher	101 Hiroji Kubota	163 Debra Schulke
18 Dieter Bauer	57 Gerrit Fokkema	102 Kaku Kurita	164 Flip Schulke
19 Nicole Bengiveno	58 Frank Fournier	103 Jean-Pierre Laffont	165 Mike Shayegani
20 P.F. Bentley	59 Roland Freeman	104 Daniel Lainé	166 Vladimir Sichov
21 Alan Berner	60 Raphaël Gaillarde	105 Xavier Lambours	167 Hans Silvester
22 Susan Biddle	61 J. Carl Ganter	106 Gov. Richard Lamm	168 Bill Simpkins
23 Alain Bizos	62 Sam Garcia	107 Jacques Langevin	169 Tom Skudra
24 Susan Bloom	63 Wilbur E. Garrett	108 Brian Lanker	170 Neal Slavin
25 Koo Bohn-Chang	64 Yves Gellie	109 Frans Lanting	171 Rick Smolan
26 Agnes Bonnot	65 Georg Gerster	110 Sarah Leen	172 Jordi Socias
27 Alex Bowie	66 John Giannini	111 Andy Levin	173 James L. Stanfield
28 Torin Boyd	67 Gianni Giansanti	112 Barry Lewis	174 Andrew Stawicki
29 David Burnett	68 Diego Goldberg	113 R. Ian Lloyd	175 George Steinmetz
30 Michele Cardon	69 Lynn Goldsmith	114 Gerd Ludwig	176 Peter Stocker
31 Dennis Chamberlin	70 Gianfranco Gorgoni	115 Jay Maisel	177 William Strode
32 Aaron Chang	71 D. Gorton	116 Pascal Maitre	178 Anthony Suau
33 Gary Chapman	72 Philip Gould	117 Mary Ellen Mark	179 Michel Szulc-Krzyzanowski
34 Paul Chesley	73 Arthur Grace	118 John Marmaras	180 Bruce Talamon
35 Luc Choquer	74 Stormi Greener	119 Adam Mastoon	181 Patrick Tehan
36 Rich Clarkson	75 Sara Grosvenor	120 Stephanie Maze	182 Tomasz Tomaszewski
37 Jodi Cobb	76 Jim Gund	121 Linda McConnell	183 Aaron Tomlinson
38 Serge Cohen	77 Carol Guzy	122 Steve McCurry	184 David Turnley
39 Sandy Colton	78 Skeeter Hagler	123 Joe McNally	185 Peter Turnley
	79 Al Harvey	124 Wally McNamee	186 Penny Tweedie
	80 David Alan Harvey	125 Dilip Mehta	187 Neal Ulevich
	81 Gregory Heisler	126 Rudi Meisel	188 Burk Uzzle
	82 Andy Hernandez	127 Michael Melford	189 Jerry Valente
	83 François Hers	128 Doug Menuez	190 John Vink
	84 Volker Hinz	129 Claus C. Meyer	191 Patrick Ward
		130 Maddy Miller	192 Ron Watts
		131 Brian Milne	193 Mark S. Wexler
		132 Yan Morvan	194 John H. White
		133 Carl Mydans	195 Joy Wolf
		134 Matthew Naythons	196 Adam Woolfitt
		135 Andy Nelson	197 Michael S. Yamashita
		136 Chris Niedenthal	198 Ian Yeomans
		137 Alain Nogues	199 Franco Zecchin
		138 Kazuyoshi Nomachi	200 Tom Zetterstrom
		139 Seny Norasingh	
		140 Koni Nordmann	
		141 Michael O'Brien	
		142 Richard Olsenius	
		143 Pablo Ortiz Monasterio	
		144 Graeme Outerbridge	
		145 Daniele Pellegrini	
		146 Mark Peters	

Skeeter Hagler

A cowboy on the Pitchfork Ranch in Guthrie, Texas.

● Seattle/187

● Sunburst/

● Portland/44

● Lewiston/47

● Richland/128

● Walla Walla/157

● Riggins/127

● Eugene/67

● Gilchrist/90

Yellowstone/109

● Boonville/64

● Reno/55

● Salt Lake City/29

● Napa Valley/63

● Sacramento Delta/22

● Ione/192

● Ely/107

● Manti/30

Marin County, Oakland/11

● San Francisco/132

● Cove Fort, Elsinore/1

● Silicon Valley/171

● Salinas, Monterey, Big Sur/52

● St. George/2

● Parkfield/58

● Grand Canyon/36

● Bakersfield/58

● Las Vegas/159

● Walpi/162

● Antelope Valley/154

● Hollywood/97

● Beverly Hills/175

● Santa Monica, Venice/165

● Los Angeles/110, 169

● East Los Angeles/88

● Phoenix/82

● Coronado/194

● Imperial Valley/148

● Tucson/100

● Green Valley/100

● Nogales/100

● Kauai/99

● Honolulu/86

● The Kona Coast/105

252

James Balog

Barrow, Alaska, the northernmost town in America.

Daniele Pellegrini

Dolly Parton greets the press before the opening of her theme park, "Dollywood," in Pigeon Fork, Tennessee.

Peter Turnley

A textile worker in Kannapolis, North Carolina.

Dan Dry

Anthony Lyvers has been curing hams for 30 years in Loretto, Kentucky.

Northwest Angle/76

Benedicta/62
Belfast/144
Mt. Desert Island/99

Minot/123

Hibbing/66
Duluth/66   White Pine/26

Mt. Washington/43
E. Topsham, Barre/149

Billings/160

Gloucester/133
Adirondacks/39   Lowell/40
Sheridan/138   Minneapolis/98   Syracuse/176   Boston/198
Devils Tower/138   Rochester/168   Providence/70
Gillette/138   New Ulm/164   Corning/61   Newport/141
La Crosse/158   Lake Huron/131   Litchfield County/23
Mt. Rushmore/103   Austin/3   Monticello/56   Bridgeport/104
Traverse City/10   Greenwich/19
Pine Ridge/45   Madison/18   Grand Rapids/28   Long Island/24, 155
Gordon/142   Detroit/31   New York City/6, 17, 37, 60, 122, 125,
Dearborn/178   166, 170, 184, 188, 195
Battle Creek/13   Cleveland/140   Harrisburg/84   Paramus/68   Asbury Park/147
Youngstown/121   Philadelphia/191
Chicago/34, 87, 180   Pittsburgh/38   Lancaster/193
Stuart/77   Weirton, Wheeling/116   Baltimore/35   Atlantic City/113
Omaha/42   Delaware/152
Palmer/130   Fairfield/135   Columbus/53   Washington, DC/8, 12, 15, 108, 139
Middleburg/197
Indianapolis/118   Smith Island/27
Springfield/81   Cincinnati/183   Charlottesville/83
Denver/21, 106, 126, 190   Cuba/156   Freedom/101   Milton/75   Cabin Creek/173
Aurora/199   Glasgow, Boonville/16   Norfolk/136
Kansas City/102   St. Louis/74   Louisville/46   Pikeville/177
Lawrence/65   East St. Louis/153   Kitty Hawk/79
Telluride/5   Garden City/89   Lebanon/181   Winston-Salem/129
Shiprock/48   Witchita/196   Cairo/33   Kannapolis/185
Gallup/48   Nashville/49   Great Smoky Mountains/145
Santa Fe/41   Tulsa/119   Fayetteville/93   Fort Mill/189
Boley, Prague/9   Gainesville/57
Albuquerque/73   Memphis/59   Huntsville/163   Charleston/32
Oxford/137   Marietta, Atlanta/20
Guthrie/78   Parris Island/91
Greenville/71   Vidalia, Soperton/182
Savannah/114
Dallas/25, 112
Big Spring/174   Natchez/115
El Paso/151   Midland/174   Crescent City/124
Odessa/174   Killeen/94
Big Lake/1   Huntsville/85   Biloxi/95
Lexington/85   Orlando/51
Austin/94   New Orleans/80, 111   Titusville/186
Luckenbach/94   Houston/4, 72   St. Petersburg/117
Mountain Home/146   New Iberia/134
Terlingua, Big Bend/200   San Antonio/172   Palm Beach/179

Miami/69, 120
The Everglades/92

Rio Grande Valley/143   Marathon/50
Key West/96

A Day in the Life of America Revisited

There is a big problem with this book, *A Day in the Life of America*. It looks too easy. You page through it, absorbed by this collective snapshot of one extraordinary country on one ordinary day, and it all appears so effortless. "Yes," you find yourself murmuring, "this is what America is." You don't find yourself thinking, "Gee, I wonder how they got these shots?"

In a way, the lack of wonder is a tribute to just how good these pictures are —and a statement of what photojournalism is all about. You know the old quote (probably first uttered by a photojournalist) about one picture being "worth a thousand words"? It's meant to be taken literally. Photographs, especially when they are taken by the best, 200 of whom spread out across this vast land on May 2, 1986, are supposed to speak for themselves. They don't require explanation. Like great magic tricks, they simply are.

But there is a story behind this particular bit of prestidigitation, one that involves months of planning, tens of thousands of work hours and the talents of a lot of extraordinary people. Since there isn't a camera handy, it will require more than a thousand words to tell it.

It begins, as most good tales do, a long time ago, way back in 1978, with a young American photojournalist named Rick Smolan who was covering an Australian woman who had taken it upon herself to trek the width of her 3,000-mile homeland via camel. (Hold on, the story gets weirder.) During the course of that assignment, Rick got a couple of improbable notions into his head. The first was that Australia was one of the most intriguing countries he had ever seen; the second was that he could convince 100 of the world's leading photojournalists to fly halfway around the planet to spend a day recording all of Down Under's wonders on film. The result, Rick figured, might make for a pretty good book.

Two dozen Australian publishers thought otherwise. They told him that no publisher in the world could afford to fund a project of that size. And they doubted these famous photographers would really take time off from their normal jobs to fly all the way to Australia to work on a one-day assignment. They also didn't think photographs taken on just one day would say anything interesting or significant about an entire country. And, most important, the publishers didn't believe the book would sell. The public would never be interested in such a "gimmicky" idea.

None of this deterred Smolan. He went ahead and, with a group of friends, spent the better part of three years lining up financial backing for the project. Finally, on March 6, 1981, the 100 photojournalists everyone said would never come, showed up right on schedule, and the world got to see just how extraordinary Australia really was. In the process, they also turned out something more than a pretty good book. Independently published by Rick and a few friends in Sydney, *A Day in the Life of Australia* sold 200,000 copies, some sort of an Australian sales record.

By now, Smolan had a partner named David Cohen, an even younger Yale graduate who had left behind the management of a New York photo agency (Contact Press Images) and the wisdom his Alma Mater allegedly imparts, to join the Australia project. "Photojournalism has to be the greatest form of delayed adolescence ever invented," says Cohen. Together Smolan and Cohen did three more *Day in the Life* books over the next four years: *A Day in the Life of Hawaii* (December 2, 1983); *A Day in the Life of Canada* (June 8, 1984); *A Day in the Life of Japan* (June 7, 1985).

This should have been enough for anyone (even Sylvester Stallone had called it quits after *Rocky IV*), and it might have been if Smolan and Cohen hadn't been so enraptured by the romance of photojournalism. But they were, and it wasn't, and so in January, 1986, Smolan, Cohen and a dozen of similarly smitten others removed themselves to Bermuda to plan their next caper. All they knew as they boarded the plane was that whatever they came up with, it would have to be the biggest thing yet or it wouldn't be worth doing.

How many batteries does this thing take? The theory was that when official group photographer Jim Balog pushed the button on his camera, all these flashes would go off. And, believe it or not, it worked— with the help of banks of Tekno Balcar strobe lights—as witnessed by the 200-plus *Day in the Life of America* photographers pictured at left.

Bag men: Project co-directors Rick Smolan and David Cohen with two hundred *Day in the Life of America* photographer kits.

Eric Lars Bakke

Eric Lars Bakke

The weather in Bermuda was lousy; in fact, tornadoes were raking the island, something that isn't supposed to happen in Bermuda. Some might have taken this as an omen. The photojournalists, in the midst of passing around a bottle or two (something their ilk is very good at), were trying to decide where to shoot next. Brazil, Italy, Ireland, China and the U.S.S.R. were all suggested, but it was the most obvious choice that the group finally settled on: It was time to bring the idea home and do America.

Smolan had his doubts. If 100 photographers were divided equally among the 50 states that would leave only two photographers to cover each state. Another problem was whether Americans would be interested in a book about the entire country—or did they just think of themselves as Californians or New Yorkers? One idea that was actually considered was to assemble 50 teams of photographers and do 51 books on the same day; one for each state and one big book with the best from all the states. Cooler heads, represented by Cohen, prevailed. "Let's just double the number of photographers to 200 and assign them according to each state's population," he suggested. In the months to come even that would prove to be a logistical nightmare.

A week after the Bermuda meeting, they called a planning session, on, as luck would have it (and they were beginning to wonder about that now), the same day as the space shuttle disaster. Among those present was Rich Clarkson, director of photography at National Geographic, who would become the director of photography for the *Day in the Life of America* (DITLA) project. To undertake the enterprise, the organizers calculated, would require the talents of no fewer than 40 staff members, a logistical team to be drawn from magazines and photo agencies all over the world. Assigning 200 photographers would entail certain logistical problems, small items such as 5000 rolls of film, 500 or so round-trip air tickets, 2000 hotel room nights, 200-plus rental cars, and maybe 20 Macintosh computers to keep track of all the etceteras. Then there was the production cost which, with top-quality, five-color printing on coated stock of a durability suitable for rafting down the Colorado River ("We want this to be on people's coffee tables 40 years from now," Smolan explained), came to a neat $4.6 million. "Hmm," they said, which was somewhat milder than the reaction of Collins Publishers, their London-based publisher.

The solution, as it had been with the other *Day in the Life* books, was to seek corporate underwriting. In all, Smolan and Cohen visited 40 companies making their pitch. "Our approach is fairly lunatic," says Cohen. "We walk into a prospective sponsor's office with 20 pounds of *Day in the*

Life books under our arms and make the following offer: 'We want your company to support a photography project that takes place on one day, a day chosen because nothing special is going to happen. It's the largest such undertaking in history, and no one's ever done it before. No, we won't put any pictures of your company's products in the book. No, we won't photograph your factory or your CEO. No, you can't see the book until it appears, and no, you can't censor anything. You just have to trust us and the photographers—and we can tell you in advance, the portrait you're going to get will be a warts-and-all look at the nation. What do you get in return? Your name on the first page, some free copies and the right to use duplicates of the pictures.' The wonder," Cohen smilingly adds, "is not that 34 companies turned us down, but that there were six that didn't."

With the finances in place, Smolan and Cohen flew to Europe and rounded up the heads of some of the world's leading photo agencies. Over a memorable dinner in Paris following the World Press Photo Awards, the editors, headed up by Robert Pledge, president of the New York–based picture agency, Contact Press Images, began thrashing through just who ought to take America's picture. (Another team led by *Geographic*'s Rich Clarkson was doing the same in New York.) There were, shall we say, a host of divergent opinions. But by the time the third round of cognac was quaffed everyone was feeling mellow. "It sounds corny," says Smolan, "but doing something that the experts say is impossible has a way of bringing creative people together. It's like having a common enemy."

One of their biggest enemies was time. In order to shoot the book and have it out in time for the Christmas season, the project would have to be shot in early spring, which at that point, was only two months away. The organizers also had to decide where to base themselves. Every book about America seemed to come out of the east or west coast. If they set up a base of operations in the center of the country, the book might have a different, more honest, look. The DITLA team ended up choosing Denver, Colorado on the basis of its allegedly superb air connections and lack of seductive diversions. The first allegation was true, the second, happily, was not.

The organizers also hoped that by basing themselves in Denver (rather than cynical San Francisco or jaded New York), the local community would take the project to heart. In fact, within days of their arrival, Dick Fleming, head of a downtown Denver business consortium, convinced the local movers-and-shakers that it would be "interesting" to host 200 lensmen from the far corners of the earth. The business community treated the *Day in the Life* staff with

The A-Team: The Denver-based DITLA core staff included (clockwise from left): Cathy Quealy (finance), Susan Duca (intern), Gillian Houston (finance), Anne Romer (film traffic), Andrée Clift (office assistant), Gae McGregor (corporate relations), Rick Smolan (co-director), Spencer Reiss (Managing Editor), David Cohen (co-director), Curt Sanburn (assignment editor), Jennifer Erwitt (production), Patti Richards (publicity), Catherine Pledge (logistics), Amy Janello (editorial), Adam Mastoon (intern), and Torin Boyd (assignment editor). Carole Bidnick (sales) was out of town trying to sell some books.

And if you don't like your assignment, talk to these folks. The DITLA assignment editors: (left to right, standing) Devyani Kamdar (West Coast), Jim Richardson (Northern Plains), Anne Day (New England), John Durniak (Middle Atlantic States), Sara Grosvenor (Upper South), Torin Boyd (Midwest), Victor Fisher (Middle Atlantic States), Shelly Katz (Southwest); (seated) Frank Johnston (Upper South), Curt Sanburn (Mountain States), D. Gorton (Deep South), Pam Abramson (West Coast), Spencer Reiss (Managing Editor).

Eric Lars Bakke

Rich Clarkson

more hospitality than they were used to, offering the free use of luxurious office space, cars, hotel rooms, meals, mobile telephones and even some local school buses to transport photographers around town.

The DITLA offices, meanwhile, were beginning to crowd with the first of what would eventually become hundreds of employees and volunteers. Now the tricky part began: convincing the 200 designated photographers that they should drop everything they were doing and join in this extravagant whimsy.

To understand how such a thing might have been contemplated, you have to know a little about photojournalists. They are, to put it gently, somewhat different from normal people. Their identifying marks, as those who have worked with them will testify, are a childlike curiosity (a fact, some would say, that derives from a stubborn refusal to grow up); a teenager's permanent pout ("Why can't I have my helicopter?"); a masochist's propensity for putting themselves in harm's way (who else would think of Beirut as a great place to spend a month?); and, among a tortured myriad of other characteristics, many endearing, a few not, an agoraphobe's aversion to working in packs, the photojournalists' term for which is unprintable in this context. There is, though, one susceptibility in these shy egomaniacs' Nikon-laden psyches: they love challenges. Would they abandon careers and assorted loved ones to come to the largest, most outlandish photo undertaking of all time? Of course they would.

The task of converting this presumption into reality was left chivalrously, as were the other chores deemed impossible by Messrs. Smolan and Cohen, to a woman. In this instance, Catherine Pledge, who in four days of nonstop telephoning lined up the magic 200 in a total of 33 foreign countries. While Catherine was developing cauliflower ear, Cathy Quealy was managing the office, which, depending on the hour of the day, resembled either a zoo, the headquarters of a political campaign or the nerve center for the invasion of an island somewhat larger than Grenada. As an Australian who had for six years run the daily life of her country's prime minister, Cathy thought this all quite normal.

On the other hand, Gae McGregor, DITLA's corporate marketing director, was thrown completely cold into the wheedling, bartering and begging of small items like 2000 free nights of hotel room accommodations, hundreds of United Airlines' tickets (try, sometime, to arrange the schedules of 200 not-notoriously reliable people scattered around the globe, so that they will arrive at the same place, on the same day at about the same hour) and all the other items without which DITLA would have been a Smolan-Cohen pipe dream.

Every time things started to get out of control (an almost daily occurrence) someone with the right skills would show up and offer to help. One such guardian angel was Karen Bakke, a professional travel agent who masochistically offered to donate a little time after work each day. "A little time," for Karen, like most of the other volunteers, turned out to occupy most of her waking hours.

Then there was the handling of the press, which (to the staff's initial delight, then slowly growing horror) had become unexpectedly captivated by the project. Patti Richards, the project's publicity director, thought DITLA would receive a fair amount of coverage when she mailed out releases to the newspapers and television stations in the towns the photojournalists would be covering, but nothing on the scale of what ultimately emerged. CBS rang up one day and mentioned they'd be doing a piece and would be dispatching 12 crews. ABC's "20/20" made a similar announcement, adding that they'd be fielding film crews from 83 ABC affiliates. Matters began to get out of hand when WQED, the PBS station that produces the *National Geographic* television specials, offered to do an hour documentary and send along 20 film crews. And the local media had yet to be heard from. When those calls started coming, from newspapers, television stations and some radio outlets no one had ever heard of —many of them wanting to cover the people who were covering the people who were covering America—a bleary-eyed Richards groaned, "This is getting out of control. It's turning into a media circus." Which, as it turned out, was precisely the case.

Paul Chesley

Rick Smolan

Heavyweight lightboxers: These top picture editors slaved over hot lightboxes looking at a quarter of a million *Day in the Life of America* photographs. They are (left to right, top to bottom) Anne Stovell of *Time*, Robert Pledge of Contact Press Images, Shirley Le Goubin of Colorific!, film traffic coordinator Anna Romer, Claudine Maugendre of *Actuel Magazine*, Susan Vermazen of *New York Magazine*, Arnold Drapkin of *Time*, Karen Mullarkey of *Newsweek*, Sandra Eisert of *The San Jose Mercury News*, Howard Chapnick of the Black Star agency, Michael Rand of *The Sunday Times Magazine*, London, Rich Clarkson of *National Geographic*, Woody Camp of Woodfin Camp and Associates, designer Leslie Smolan of Carbone Smolan Associates, Christian Caujolle of *Liberation*, Eliane Laffont of the Sygma Agency, Dieter Steiner of *Stern* and John Durniak.

How many Pulitzer Prize winners does it take to screw in a flash bulb? Nine were on hand for *A Day in the Life of America*. They were: (standing) Larry Price of *The Philadelphia Inquirer*, Neal Ulevich of the Associated Press, Carol Guzy of *The Miami Herald*, former White House photographer David Hume Kennerly, Jay Dickman of the *Dallas Times Herald*, Bill Strode; (kneeling) Tony Suau of Black Star, Skeeter Hagler of *The Dallas Times Herald* and John White of the *Chicago Sun-Times*.

National exposure: *National Geographic* photographer Jodi Cobb took a break from her DITLA assignment on New York's Fifth Avenue to make a quick appearance on the *Today Show*.

Out of the frying pan, into the refrigerator: After a tense morning shooting the group portrait (page 254), Jim Balog headed off to his assignment on the northern coast of Alaska.

Funny, it doesn't look like Arizona: Jim Brandenburg and Kent Kobersteen of *National Geographic* missed their DITLA assignments when they were suddenly called off to the North Pole to cover a dogsled expedition. The editors never got to see what Kobersteen would have shot in Arizona, but they did get this nice shot of the boys wearing *Day in the Life of America* T-shirts at the pole.

There is a pose in Spanish Harlem: David Turnley spent his *Day in the Life of America* on Manhattan's 125th Street.

With shoot day only a few weeks away, the empty room behind the DITLA offices was rapidly beginning to look like the warehouse in the final scene of *Raiders of the Lost Ark*. Under the meticulous supervision of production director Jennifer Erwitt, crates of film, cooler bags, caption books, film envelopes and 200 underwater cameras were turned into individual kits for each photographer. In addition to the necessities, many of the sponsors had donated gifts and assorted paraphernalia with their names adorning them. At one point David Cohen walked into the DITLA office simultaneously sporting three caps (Kodak, Nikon, Merrill Lynch), a Banana Republic vest, a United Airlines flight jacket, a Kodak T shirt, an Apple computer note pad and an underwater Nikon camera around his neck. "Anyone think that maybe these projects are getting a little too commercial?" Cohen asked the amused staff.

Other people were keeping busy, too, and few more so than Spencer Reiss of *Newsweek*, who was doing detached duty as DITLA's managing editor. "This project," he explained, "is like a kid's connect-the-dots puzzle, with the photographers as the dots. When you draw a line between all the dots, you end up with a picture of America. The trick is putting the dots in the right place."

Doing that was the chore of DITLA's nine assignment editors, who, aided by assistant managing editor Amy Janello, on loan from American Showcase, fanned out over the country to reconnoiter the terrain. One of them, former New York Timesman D. Gorton, spent a month traversing the Deep South by car, drinking in small town bars, scouting up lonely country lanes, painstakingly mapping out the ground over which his photographers would travel ("Smelling the docks," he called it with a distinctly Mississippi twang) and, along the way, lining up accommodations so the photojournalists would have a taste of living with typical American families.

Gorton also spent his time on the road listening to his AM car radio, alert for the crackle of Americana. Driving through rural Georgia one night, he knew he'd heard the

genuine article, a fiery black radio preacher named Tim Hicks. When he called the reverend at his church, explained the project and asked if he might impose on May 2nd with a photojournalist trailed by half a dozen newspaper and television reporters, the preacher told Gorton to come on ahead. "God," he said, "has sent you to me."

Whose side the Lord was really on came briefly into question when, only a few days before the photographers pulled into Denver, there was another of those omens—the Chernobyl nuclear plant exploded—and, with it, came momentary panic. "My God," said Cohen, "what if the Russians give all our photographers visas? We'll lose all of them." Fortunately, the Russians stayed Russian and the crisis passed.

Not so easily fixed were several more mundane problems, like the fact that, thanks to the unexpected arrival of a convention of neurosurgeons, Denver's hotels were solidly booked (Sheraton eventually solved that by donating to DITLA most of an entire hotel on the outskirts of town). Also, courtesy of a transatlantic screw-up, 40 French photojournalists were cooling their heels in the Orly departure lounge, *sans billet d'avion*. With a lot of oaths and late night phone calls to DITLA's Paris agent, Annie Boulat, that glitch, too, was worked out, and the clan was on its way.

As their flights arrived, the photographers were met at the airport by staff members carrying huge *Day in the Life of America* banners. (Anyone carrying a camera bag at Stapleton International airport in Denver was assumed by the staff to be a DITLA photographer—an assumption which led to some embarassing scenes.) For the next few days, before they headed off to their assignments, the photographers would be briefed on their assignments, outfitted with their film and other paraphernalia and scared silly by the awesome competition. On the final evening, culminating three days of camaraderie, a game of Photon (a high-tech version of "capture the flag" where players dress in blinking space suits and run around shooting harmless laser guns at each other in a dark maze filled with mist) caused an impolitic moment when photographer Yuri Abramochkin, of the Soviet Union, was asked to captain the "red team." He accepted gracefully.

Janice Rubin

Giddy-up, comrade: Although it was a long ride from Moscow, Soviet photographer Yuri Abramochkin fit right in deep in the heart of Texas. Texas Governor Mark White declared him an honorary Texas citizen.

Misha Erwitt

They shoot on horsey-back, don't they? Roland Freeman gives a budding young photographer a boost and a few tips at the Kodak Children's Workshop in Denver.

Leslie Smolan

Adams' eve: Eddie Adams took time out for a quick interview with the *NBC Evening News* during his assignment in Telluride, Colorado.

Vern Iuppa

Swiss cheesecake: Francois Robert of Switzerland photographed these ladies of the night at a Las Vegas brothel.

The next morning, before the photographers boarded planes to their assignments, John Durniak, former picture editor of *The New York Times*, gave them a last pep talk. "Friday is May 2nd," he intoned. "Shoot the hell out of the country."

Shoot the hell out of it they did, with, as you have witnessed, astounding results. Which brings us back to that question: "How did they get those shots?"

At the risk of disturbing some of the magic, the answer was a trifle more involved than being in the right place at the right time with the right light and lens opening—though, certainly, that didn't hurt.

There were, in the first place, some technical difficulties to overcome. Photojournalist Jay Dickman, for instance, found himself atop New Hampshire's Mt. Washington, site of some of the worst weather in the world, in the midst of 90 m.p.h. winds and severe sub-zero fog. That didn't bother him so much as not knowing what lens filter to use in mercury vapor lighting. A quick call to Nikon, which had set up a complete camera clinic for DITLA in Denver, straightened him out.

Nature, in the form of Idaho's Salmon River, also caused problems for Michael Melford, who spent an hour white-water rafting ("It was cold and wet, miserable; I turned blue"). In the form of high winds, it caused problems for Chris Johns, who photographed Garden City, Kansas from a crop duster. "It was kind of hairy flying," says Johns. "We were getting knocked around quite a bit. Any other day, I wouldn't have done it. But that was the job and I thought it was important to do it."

In other cases, the hazards were man-made. Australian photojournalist Gerrit Fokkema, who drew the assignment of photographing the Georgia Ku Klux Klan, turned up unannounced at the Gainesville, Georgia, home of the "Grand Titan" to find him on his front lawn, hand clutched on a pearl-handled revolver. Back-up artillery, in the form of a submachine gun, was in the house. "He said he was ready to use it," Fokkema recalls. "It was quite sobering."

In Spanish Harlem, David Turnley was accosted by an indignant resident ("A big strong guy, who looked like he was into lifting weights") with two giant Great Danes on leash. "He said I didn't belong there, and I shouldn't be taking pictures without permission," says Turnley. "He came right up to my face. His dogs were sniffing my crotch. I looked him straight in the eye and didn't back off. Finally, he drifted away. He didn't want to fight anymore than I did."

By and large, however, the DITLA photojournalists were struck by the friendliness of their subjects; indeed, of everyone they encountered. Roger Ressmeyer, who nearly had his hair singed photographing the take-off of a Mach-3, SR-71 "Blackbird" at Edwards Air Force Base, gushed, "I couldn't believe how excited people were about this project. I've been treated well before, but the Air Force and NASA people were falling all over themselves. It was like everyone was excited, almost proud, of being part of *A Day in the Life of America*. Generals were meeting me at the gate, taking me places. It was phenomenal, wonderful. I'd never experienced anything like it."

At times, the reception was so effusive the photojournalists had trouble working. Ben Fernandez, who photographed Columbus, Ohio, had his picture on the front page of the local newspaper and was trailed by fans seeking his autograph. "Instead of sneaking around quietly doing my reportage," recounts Fernandez, "I wound up being a celebrity."

No one asked Nina Barnett for her autograph, but Barnett, who covered life along the Missouri River, was also struck by American cordiality. "Usually I meet with aggression when I ask to take a person's picture," she says. "But not May 2nd. I was truly amazed how unparanoid the people were that day. They accepted me as a photographer and welcomed me into their homes. They were very proud of their lives."

Film star: President Reagan took his *Day in the Life of America* photographs on board Air Force One—halfway between a meeting with Indonesian President Suharto on Bali and an economic summit with free world leaders in Tokyo.

Yeah, but, who's flying the plane? When the President of the United States said, "Smile," Air Force One went on autopilot.

Picture book romance: German photojournalist Gerd Ludwig met L.A. photographer Dana Fineman on the *Day in the Life of Hawaii* project (1983), romanced her during the *Day in the Life of Canada* project (1984) and married her in Denver right after the *Day in the Life of America* shoot.

Caption Courageous: *National Geographic* ace David Alan Harvey was still trying to caption over 50 rolls of film (1,800 shots) just before deadline.

The foreign contingent was especially impressed. "It was an extraordinary experience," says French photojournalist Jean-Pierre Laffont, who photographed Mount Rushmore. "The people were absolutely fantastic. I had my picture taken, I was on the TV, there was an article about me in the newspaper. I even lived in a log cabin, and during the night I could hear deer running all around."

"In my country," adds Italian photographer Franco Zecchin, who put aside his usual pastime photographing the Sicilian Mafia to document life in the sprawling suburb of Aurora, Colorado, "the people are very suspicious of photojournalists, especially the Mafia. You have to shoot from a distance, and, in Palermo, it is very hard and very dangerous. They killed one photographer. But here, all people say yes."

Overwhelmingly, that was true. In Washington, where Congress has sharp strictures prohibiting photography in either chamber, the Senate passed a special resolution allowing James K.W. Atherton to snap away to his heart's content. Up Pennsylvania Avenue, the doors were also open at the White House. An hour before announcing to the world that the U.S. had bombed Libya, presidential spokesman Larry Speakes had taken the time with assignment editor Frank Johnston to arrange for Ronald Reagan to participate in *A Day in the Life of America* by asking him to take pictures aboard Air Force One. In Oklahoma, where Adam Mastoon shot the Tulsa Tribune and the evangelical empire of the Roberts, Oral and Richard, the way was greased with the passage of a state proclamation declaring May 2nd to be *A Day in the Life of America* Day in the Sooner State. Texas, not to be outdone, did the same. In suburban Long Island, a Jewish synagogue opened its doors Passover Friday for REZA, a Moslem photojournalist from Iran. A mosque in suburban Detroit did the same thing for Roman Catholic photojournalist (and Pulitzer Prize winner) Tony Suau.

But if, to quote a Smolanism, "nine-tenths of photojournalism is talking your way past the palace guards and one-tenth pushing the button," there were some palace guards, and some subjects, more resistant than others. In New York, for instance, Indian photojournalist Dilip Mehta found Mayor Ed Koch in an uncharacteristically grumpy mood. "You can have 60 seconds," hizzoner growled. "No, no, that's 30 seconds too much," Mehta smiled back, and, with that, led Koch outside and handed him an apple. Charmed, Koch grinned and tossed the apple in the air.

On the "Space Coast" of eastern Florida, Australian Penny Tweedie turned up at a local aerospace plant the same day that 360 people were being laid off—a fact that did not put the "little, rat-like security people" in a particularly good humor. "Everywhere I went," says Tweedie "the security guys would be rushing around in front of me, saying 'Don't let her photograph you. Don't sign any model releases. There shouldn't be a photographer here.' The irony was that the people who were being fired didn't mind being photographed. They were only too happy to have their pictures taken."

On New York's Fifth Avenue, Jodi Cobb, who had been interviewed about the project that morning on the *Today* show, discovered a chic shop manager incensed over her remarks. "He was shouting how he wouldn't let me shoot because I had said something on the *Today* show about Fifth Avenue not being my first choice of assignment. He said I didn't really want to be there and he didn't want to let me in. 'America is power, America is money,' he said. 'America is not bums on the street,' which, according to him, is what I wanted to shoot. I joked with him, 'You should have seen the part the *Today* show cut, about the vitality and spirit of Fifth Avenue.' From then on, it all went fine. The guy was dying to have me shoot him, but he just needed a little coaxing."

Across the continent, in Juneau, Alaska, Donna Ferrato arrived to spend the night at the governor's mansion and accidently found a note left for the housekeeper. "Natalie," it read, "tonight this woman named Donna Ferrato will be arriving to spend the night in the mansion. Now, understand this, she is just a photographer, she is to have no special favors bestowed on her. She is to be shown up to her room immediately and the doors shut, so she can't get down to the second floor, where the governor sleeps. Remember, no special favors."

Karen, will you marry us? When *Newsweek* picture editor Karen Mullarkey caught the bouquet at the Fineman-Ludwig wedding, she was besieged by suitors—including DITLA project organizer David Cohen, Pulitzer Prize winner Eddie Adams and top corporate photographer Jay Maisel.

Pressed for time: Designers Tom Walker and Leslie Smolan of Carbone Smolan Associates working around the clock during printing in Japan.

By the end of the 24 hours that was May 2nd, nearly all the photographers got their pictures anyway. Some, like Stephanie Maze, who photographed Miami's "Little Havana," had been moved by the experience ("I had tears in my eyes when I was shooting Cuban senior citizens dancing, the spirit of it was beautiful"); others, like Susan Duca, who had photographed the down-and-out in Lewiston, Idaho, discomforted ("Sometimes, I had to stop shooting; the things I saw were so sad"), while a few, like Andy Levin, who spent the day in a New Orleans' emergency room, wished they hadn't seen the things they had ("Having to work with people who are in pain and asking them to let me take their picture and sign releases, was too intense. I wouldn't do it again.") All, however, had taken away a part of America, and a new understanding of it. "I didn't know what was really out there before," said Eddie Adams, the Pulitzer Prize-winning photojournalist whose photograph of a street-corner execution of a Viet Cong suspect helped change the course of the war. "I didn't know America was so beautiful. See, I don't go to the beautiful places; we all go to the rough spots where the assignments are. But today it was different, and it freaked me out. I got so overwhelmed, I didn't know what to do. Everything was so awesome. I couldn't decide what to shoot. One day isn't enough. I have to go back."

When the photographers finished shooting, they flew back to Denver to turn in their film. With tape recorders and questionnaires in hand, several picture editors, organized by Rita Jacobs, debriefed the photographers. Afterwards there was a farewell party which had a special feel to it. Two of the photographers who had met while working on the *Day in the Life of Hawaii* project in 1983, Dana Fineman from Los Angeles and Gerd Ludwig from West Germany, had decided to get married and invited all 200 photographers to be their guests at what turned out to be the most photographed wedding since Prince Charles married Lady Di in Westminster Abbey.

The next morning, the photographers boarded planes and headed back to their normal jobs. For them DITLA was over. For Rick and David and their friends the real work was just beginning. It was a staggering load: 245,000 pictures had been shot altogether, by far the largest number of photographs that had ever been taken on one day of any single subject. They had set a record—and they had also caused themselves one helluva problem. How in the world were they going to whittle it down to a single book?

The answer lay in 18 picture editors from leading picture agencies and magazines like *Newsweek, Time, National Geographic* and *New York Magazine* who went through the horde, voting each picture in or out. They found some surprising omissions—no pictures of fast-food outlets, for instance, apparently because each photographer assumed one of the other 199 would get it—and some equally surprising duplications, such as the fact that six photojournalists, acting independently, had turned in pictures of high school proms. They also discovered that, in a number of instances, the photojournalists had "gone off the reservation," abandoning their scheduled assignments to shoot subjects of their own whim and choosing. These, it turned out, included some of the best pictures of all.

After several weeks of 18-hour days, the pile had shrunk to a select 850 frames. These were handed over to Leslie Smolan, DITLA's long-time designer and a partner in Carbone Smolan Associates, one of New York City's leading design firms. Working together with associate art director Tom Walker, Leslie was able to compress what would have normally taken 15 months of work into five weeks of late nights. Following a final run-through for photo agency heads and photo editors, the writing of captions and the engagement of one of those (sniff) "word people" to explain how it all came to be, the entire package was shipped off to the printer. The result—and we trust it will be on your coffee table 40 years from now—you hold in your hands.

Would they do it again, the duo of Smolan and Cohen, who are looking a little hollow-eyed these days? "Never," they vow.

That, you should be warned, is what they said after Australia.

—Robert Sam Anson

Photographers' Biographies

Sam Abell
American/Washington, D.C.
Born in Ohio, Abell learned his photography skills at home from his father. Since 1970 Abell has been a contract photographer for *National Geographic*.

Mike Abrahams
British/London
Abrahams has been a working photographer in London for the past 11 years. His work has appeared in *The Times* (London), *The Sunday Times* (London), *The Observer* and *Sunday Express*. He is a founding member of the Network Agency.

Yuri Abramochkin
Soviet/Moscow
Born in Moscow in 1936, Abramochkin began working as a photographer for the Novosti press in 1961. His book, *Photographs by Yuri Abramochkin*, will appear in 1986. He considers photography to be a universal language and the most truthful means of conveying information.

Saigon   1969

Eddie Adams
American/New York, New York
Winner of the Pulitzer Prize and the Silver Prix Award of the Advertising Association of Japan, Adams is one of the most decorated and published photographers in America with over 500 awards to his credit. He has photographed leaders in all fields, from the heads of state to the superstars of film, sport and high fashion.

National Geographic   1985

William Albert Allard
American/Washington, D.C.
A former staff photographer for *National Geographic*, Allard's work has also appeared in *Life*, *Sports Illustrated* and *GEO*. His award-winning study of cowboy life in the American West, *Vanishing Breed*, was published by the New York Graphic Society in 1982. In 1983 he received the American Society of Magazine Photographers' Outstanding Achievement Award.

Yann Arthus-Bertrand
French/Paris
Famous for his photographs of lions in the Masai Mara reserve, Arthus-Bertrand lived in Kenya for three years. The author of five books, his work appears regularly in *Figaro*, *GEO* and *Newlook*.

James K. W. Atherton
American/Washington, D.C.
Six-time winner of the first prize in the White House Press Photographers Association competition, Atherton is a staff photographer for *The Washington Post*. His long career has included jobs with Acme Newspictures and United Press International. He is a member of the standing committee of the Senate Press Photographer's Gallery.

Daniel Aubry
American/New York, New York
After careers in film, real estate and tourism, Aubry turned to photography in mid-life. He has acquired a far ranging list of editorial and corporate clients, among them *Connoisseur*, *GEO*, *The New York Times*, *Cosmopolitan* and Sotheby's.

José Azel
Cuban/New York, New York
Before moving to New York in 1982, Azel was a staff photographer with *The Miami Herald*. He is currently a regular contributor to Contact Press Images and has covered the 1984 Summer Olympics, Pope John Paul II's South America visit and the 1984 Democratic and Republican conventions.

Robert Azzi
American/New York, New York
Azzi has published his work in *National Geographic*, *Life* and *GEO* and has worked for many corporate clients, especially in the Middle East. He was a Nieman Fellow at Harvard and is currently represented by Woodfin Camp and Associates.

Senator Howard Baker
American/Washington, D.C.
Senator Baker represented Tennessee for 18 years in the United States Senate. Since retiring from the Senate in 1985, he has been practicing law in Washington, D.C. He has always regarded photography as his passion.

Eric Lars Bakke
American/Denver, Colorado
Bakke was most recently honored at the 1985 Pictures of the Year/ University of Missouri competition with an honorable mention for news picture story. His other awards include *The Sporting News* Best Sports Picture 1984 and 1985 and first-place feature photography in 1977 from Suburban Newspapers of America.

James Balog
American/Denver, Colorado
A frequent contributor to *National Geographic*, *Smithsonian* and Time-Life publications, Balog also does a good deal of corporate work. The International Center of Photography recently published his book, *Wildlife Requiem*.

Micha Bar-Am
Israeli/Jerusalem
A photographic correspondent for *The New York Times* since 1968, Bar-Am has published and exhibited his work the world over. During 1985-86 he was a Nieman Fellow at Harvard University.

Nina Barnett
American/New York, New York
Formerly an art production editor in publishing, Barnett is currently a freelance photographer.

Letizia Battaglia
Italian/Palermo
A staff photographer for *L'Ora*, Battaglia also publishes her work in Italian and international magazines. In 1985 she won the prestigious Eugene Smith Grant to continue her work documenting the Mafia in Sicily.

Dieter Bauer
German/Bonn
Bauer has been a professional photographer since 1973. For ten years he worked as a staff photographer for a variety of daily newspapers in Germany, and since 1983 he has been on the staff of *Stern* magazine.

New York   1986

Nicole Bengiveno
American/San Francisco, California
Named Photographer of the Year in 1979 by the San Francisco Bay Area Press Photographers Association, Bengiveno has been a staff photographer for the *San Francisco Examiner* since 1977. In 1983 she won first place in the Associated Press sports photo contest, and in 1985 she was a finalist for the Eugene Smith Award for her work on the AIDS epidemic.

P. F. Bentley
American/San Francisco, California
Bentley is a *Time* magazine contract photographer. For his comprehensive coverage of the 1984 presidential campaigns, he won first and second place in the U. S. Pictures of the Year competition.

Washington   1985

Alan Berner
American/Seattle, Washington
With an A.B. in philosophy, Berner worked for five newspapers before joining the staff of the *Seattle Times*. He has been a graphics editor and picture editor, and while at the *Arizona Daily Star* he won a Robert F. Kennedy Journalism Award for Outstanding Coverage of the Disadvantaged.

Susan Biddle
American/Denver, Colorado
A staff photographer for *The Denver Post* since 1983, Biddle has freelanced for a variety of publications and agencies including Sipa Press and Associated Press. Her career as a photographer began as director of photography for the Peace Corps.

Alain Bizos
French/Paris
Bizos was trained as a painter at the National School of Fine Arts in Paris, and in 1974 he became a founding member of *Liberation*. He has covered the world from Afghanistan to Lebanon to South America, and he has had several one-man shows. He is a member of the VU agency.

Agnes Bonnot
French/Paris
A member of the VU agency, Bonnot has been a professional photographer since 1982. She has worked regularly for *Liberation* and other magazines on portraits, landscapes and fashion shows. Her book, *Horses*, was published in 1985.

Saudi Arabia   1976

Alex Bowie
British/Manila
Bowie has freelanced from London and Madrid, covering assignments in Europe, Central America, the Middle East, East Africa and Southeast Asia for major international publications. He is a contributor to the Time-Life book series, *The Vietnam Experience*.

Torin Boyd
American/New York, New York
Boyd has worked as a news photographer for United Press International and the *Orlando Sentinel*. His pictures have appeared in *The New York Times*, *USA Today*, *Rocky Mountain News*, *Asahi Shinbun* and the *San Francisco Examiner*, among others.

David Burnett
American/New York, New York
A founding member of Contact Press Images, Burnett is the winner of many awards for photojournalism. He has covered such diverse subjects as the Iranian revolution, political developments in the Philippines, Korea, Portugal and Yugoslavia, Sadat's Egypt and Cambodian refugees in Thailand. In 1980 he was named Photographer of the Year by the National Press Photographers Association, and in 1985 he won the Olivier Rebbot Award from the Overseas Press Club.

Michele Cardon
American/Columbia, Missouri
After interning at such papers as *The Palm Beach Post* and the *Utica Observer-Dispatch*, Cardon now works for *The Orange County Register* in California.

Dennis Chamberlin
American/Denver, Colorado
A staff photographer for *The Denver Post* since 1983, Chamberlin was a member of the staff of the *Fort Wayne News-Sentinel* that was awarded a Pulitzer Prize in 1983. His work has appeared in *National Geographic Traveler*.

Aaron Chang
American/San Diego, California
Since 1979 Chang has been senior staff photographer for *Surfing* magazine. In 1982 he received the American Society of Magazine Photographers Award of Excellence and was named one of the five best sports photographers in the U.S. by *American Photographer*. His work has appeared in *Stern*, *American Photographer*, *Gentleman's Quarterly*, French *Vogue* and *People*.

Gary Chapman
American/Louisville, Kentucky
Chapman is currently a staff photographer for *The Louisville Courier-Journal Sunday Magazine*. His work has appeared in *National Geographic Traveler*, *Time*, *Forbes* and *Newsweek*.

GEO magazine   1980

Paul Chesley
American/Aspen, Colorado
As a freelance photographer with the National Geographic Society since 1975, Chesley has traveled regularly to Europe and Asia. Solo exhibitions of his work have appeared at museums in London, Tokyo and New York. His work has also appeared in *Fortune*, *Time*, *Esquire*, *GEO* and *Stern*.

Luc Choquer
French/Paris
For four years Choquer directed a project which dealt with young delinquents and drug addicts. Since 1980 he has worked mainly as a photographer covering stories for *GEO*, *Stern*, *Actuel*, *Time* and *Vanity Fair*. In 1985 he won the Prix Kodak de la Critique. He is associated with the VU agency.

Rich Clarkson
American/Washington, D.C.
Clarkson is currently director of photography for *National Geographic* and a contributing photographer to *Sports Illustrated*. He was president of the National Press Photographers Association and has twice served as chairman of the Pictures of the Year competition. He has co-authored four books, and his work has appeared in *Life*, *Time* and the *Saturday Evening Post*, among others.

A Day in the Life of Japan   1985

Jodi Cobb
American/Washington, D.C.
With a master's degree from the University of Missouri, Cobb has been a staff photographer for *National Geographic* since 1977. She has photographed major articles on China, Jerusalem, Jordan and London, and in 1985 she was named the first woman White House Photographer of the Year. She was the subject of the PBS documentary "On Assignment."

Serge Cohen
French/Paris
Cohen worked briefly for Sipa Press and French newspapers before beginning his work for major German newspapers. He is currently based in Paris and works for *Frankfurter Allgemeine* magazine and several corporations.

Sandy Colton
American/Gloversville, New York
After a long and distinguished career, Colton retired in 1984 from his position as director of photography for the Associated Press. Earlier in his career he spent 13 years in Asia as a writer and chief photographer for *Pacific Stars and Stripes* and several years as picture editor of the *Washington Star*. He writes a syndicated photo column, "Camera Angles," for the AP.

Anne Day
American/New York, New York
Day has a particular interest in architecture, and she has published three books in W.W. Norton's Classical Art and Architecture Series. Her work has also appeared in *Fortune*, *Newsweek*, *The New York Times*, *Avenue* and *Le Monde*.

A Day in the Life of Australia   1981

Arnaud de Wildenberg
French/Paris
A freelance photographer since 1984, de Wildenberg is best known for his coverage of the Afghanistan crisis and Iranian and Cambodian refugees. He won the *Paris-Match* contest for the best news report in 1980 from Uganda and an award from the World Press Photo Foundation for his coverage of Lech Walesa of Poland.

William DeKay
Canadian/Washington, D.C.
While studying at Ryerson Polytechnical Institute in Toronto, DeKay worked for several Canadian newspapers, primarily *The London Free Press*. Recently he was the first Canadian to serve as an intern for *National Geographic*. He has been published in *National Geographic*, *U.S. News and World Report*, *MacLean's* and *Science Digest*.

Jay Dickman
American/Dallas, Texas
Winner of both a 1983 Pulitzer Prize and first place in the World Press Photo of Holland competition, Dickman has been a professional photographer in Dallas for 16 years. His work has appeared in *National Geographic*, *Geo*, *Life*, *Time*, *Newsweek*, *Bunte* and *Stern*.

Portugal   1979

Pascal Dolemieux
French/Paris
Since 1981 Dolemieux has been a freelance photographer for many magazines and newspapers, particularly *Liberation*. He worked with Minister of Culture Jack Lang for 10 months and has exhibited in the Bibliotheque Nationale and the National Center for Photography in Paris. In 1983 he received the Prix Niepce. He works with the VU agency.

Don Doll, S.J.
American/Omaha, Nebraska
Chairman of the Fine and Performing Arts Department at Creighton University, Doll has photographed extensively on the Rosebud Reservation in South Dakota. In 1976 he received special recognition in the World Understanding category of the Pictures of the Year competition. His work has appeared in *USA Today*, *The Seattle Times* and *National Geographic*.

A Day in the Life of Hawaii   1983

Dan Dry
American/Louisville, Kentucky
Dry is a freelance photographer for *National Geographic* and other national and international publications including *Time*, *Newsweek*, *Town and Country* and *Sport*. He has won more than 300 awards, and his newspaper work was recognized by the National Press Photographers Association when he was named Newspaper Photographer of the Year in 1981.

Stephane Duroy
French/Paris
After studying law at Nanterre University, Duroy chose a career in photography. He worked for nine years in Great Britain and is currently working on a project on the city of Berlin. His work appears frequently in *Stern*.

Tsuneo Enari
Japanese/Kanagawa
Enari worked as a photographer for the *Mainichi Shimbun* in Tokyo from 1962 to 1974 and has worked in both New York and Los Angeles. He has followed postwar subjects such as Japanese women married to American military men and Japanese war orphans abandoned in China.

Jennifer Erwitt
American/San Francisco, California
Erwitt served as production director for the Day in the Life projects in Hawaii, Canada, Japan and America. Her photographs have appeared in all four books. Her work has also been featured in the *New York Daily News* and *Frets* magazine.

Misha Erwitt
American/New York, New York
A native New Yorker, Erwitt has been taking pictures since he was 11 and is now on the staff of one of his hometown papers, the *New York Daily News*. Erwitt has been published in *American Photographer*, *Esquire*, *People*, *Manhattan, Inc.* and *USA Today*.

Miguel Luis Fairbanks
American/Columbia, Missouri
Fairbanks has served internships in photography at *The Miami Herald*, *San Jose Mercury News* and *National Geographic*.

Ben Fernandez
American/New York, New York
Presently chairman of the Photography Department at the New School for Social Research/Parsons School of Design in New York, Fernandez studied photography with Minor White and Richard Avedon.

Terry Ferrante
American/New York, New York
Ferrante specializes in studio still-life photography for corporate clients such as *Newsweek*, Germaine Monteil, Black and Decker, Seiko watches, AT&T and Avon.

Donna Ferrato
American/New York, New York
Ferrato is the winner of one of photojournalism's most coveted prizes, the W. Eugene Smith Grant, for her documentation of domestic violence. She is associated with the Visions agency and has been published in *Fortune*, *Forbes*, *The New York Times*, *Esquire*, *GEO*, *Bunte*, *Stern* and *Attenzione*.

Dana Fineman
American/New York, New York
Fineman studied at the Art Center College of Design in Pasadena and worked for several years as an assistant to celebrity photographer Douglas Kirkland. Her work appears frequently in *Time, Newsweek* and *New York Magazine.* On May 4, 1986, she married Gerd Ludwig at the Denver Center for the Performing Arts; over 200 *A Day in the Life of America* photojournalists covered the event.

Victor Fisher
Canadian/Toronto, Ontario
Fisher served as logistics director for *A Day in the Life of Japan.* Following his studies at Ryerson Polytechnical Institute, he worked for Masterfile, Canada's top stock photography agency. Fisher's work has appeared in *Interview* magazine, among others.

Gerrit Fokkema
Australian/Sydney
Fokkema works for the *Sydney Morning Herald* and is currently the chief photographer for the Saturday color supplement, *Good Weekend.* His work is included in the collection of the Australian National Gallery.

Frank Fournier
French/New York, New York
Fournier's work has appeared in a broad array of magazines and journals including *Paris-Match, Forbes, Le Figaro, Time* and *The New York Times Magazine.* He won the 1986 World Press Photo Premier Award for Press Photo of the Year and first prize in the spot news category. He is a member of Contact Press Images.

Roland Freeman
American/Washington, D.C.
Freeman's personal work has focused mainly on the rural and urban life of black Americans. He has received grants from the National Endowment for the Humanities and the National Endowment for the Arts. His latest book is *Southern Roads/ City Pavements.*

Raphael Gaillarde
French/Paris
Gaillarde is a Gamma news photographer. His in-depth coverage of world events has appeared in many European magazines, including *GEO.*

Honolulu 1983

J. Carl Ganter
American/Evanston, Illinois
Ganter worked on *A Day in the Life of Hawaii* in 1983 while still a sophomore at Northwestern. He has since been published in *Time, The London Sunday Times Magazine* and *Nikon World.* He is an associate member of Contact Press Images.

Sam Garcia
American/New York, New York
Garcia is in charge of special projects for Nikon Technical and Professional Services. He has covered the Indianapolis 500, three Olympics, the Kentucky Derby and several NASA launches. He also trained shuttle astronauts to use Nikon 35mm equipment. His favorite assignment was covering the North Magnetic Pole in the Arctic for *A Day in the Life of Canada.*

Wilbur E. Garrett
American/Washington, D.C.
The editor of *National Geographic,* Garrett is also a working photographer who has won many awards. Among his honors are the Newhouse Citation from Syracuse University, the Distinguished Service in Journalism Award from the University of Missouri Press and the Overseas Press Club and White House Photographers awards for outstanding photography.

Yves Gellie
French/Paris
After studying medicine for eight years and practicing for one year in Africa, Gellie turned to photojournalism in 1978. He has worked for Sipa Press and *Figaro* magazine. He is currently with the Gamma Agency.

Georg Gerster
Swiss/Zurich
Gerster received a Ph.D. in German literature and philology from the University of Zurich and has been a freelance writer-photographer specializing in science since 1956. He has traveled the world and frequently contributes to *National Geographic, Neue Zurcher Zeitung, The London Sunday Times Magazine* and *Omni.*

Gianni Giansanti
Italian/Rome
Winner of a World Press Award in 1979, Giansanti has covered terrorism and conflicts in Lebanon and Poland as well as Pope John Paul II's journeys. His work is published in the major international magazines such as *Newsweek, Time, Paris-Match* and *Epoca.*

Diego Goldberg
Argentine/Buenos Aires
After beginning his photographic career in Latin America as a correspondent for Camera Press, Goldberg moved to Paris in 1977 as a Sygma staff photographer. In 1980 he moved to New York and in 1985 he returned to Argentina. His work has been featured in the world's major magazines, and in 1984 he won a World Press Photo Foundation prize for feature photography.

Montserrat 1981

Lynn Goldsmith
American/New York, New York
Goldsmith's work has appeared on the covers of *Life, Newsweek, Rolling Stone* and *People.* Among her honors are awards from the World Press Photo competition and gold, silver and bronze medals won at the International Film and Television Festival in New York. She is the founding member of LGI Photo Agency, which specializes in contemporary personality portraiture.

Gianfranco Gorgoni
Italian/New York, New York
Gorgoni frequently photographs rebels, artists and political figures. His work has appeared in *L'Espresso, Life* and *Time.* He is currently working on his fourth book, which is about Fidel Castro and Cuba. He is a founding member of Contact Press Images.

D. Gorton
American/Cincinnati, Ohio
Gorton has been the chief photographer for *The Philadelphia Inquirer* and has served on *The New York Times* staff in New York and Washington.

Philip Gould
American/Lafayette, Louisiana
A freelance photographer since 1978, Gould has produced two books, *Les Cadiens d'Asteur— Today's Cajuns* and *Louisiana, A Land Apart.* He has worked for *National Geographic Traveler, GEO, Time, Newsweek, Louisiana Life Magazine* and other international publications.

Arthur Grace
American/Washington, D.C.
Grace's most recent work includes coverage of Pope John Paul II's return to Poland, the 1983 World Cup races and a book of personal photographs. His photos have appeared in *Time, Life, Look, Newsweek, The Sunday Times* (London), and *Paris-Match.* He is currently a staff photographer for *Newsweek* in Washington.

Stormi Greener
American/Minneapolis, Minnesota
A 1985 Pulitzer finalist, Greener has worked for the *Minneapolis Star and Tribune* since 1977. Her photographs have won many awards including the Oscar Barnack Award and several World Press Association awards. She has also worked for *Newsweek* and *Stern* and for corporate publications.

Sara Grosvenor
American/Washington, D.C.
Recently based in Hong Kong as a correspondent for The Dow Jones News Service, Grosvenor's work has appeared in magazines, newspapers and in *National Geographic* Special Publications.

Jim Gund
American/Phoenix, Arizona
For two years before becoming a freelance sports photographer, Gund was a staff photographer for the *Mesa Tribune.*

Carol Guzy
American/Miami, Florida
One week before working on *A Day in the Life of America* Guzy won the 1986 Pulitzer Prize for photography. She has worked for *The Miami Herald* since 1980. Her various assignments range from the Ethiopian famine to the 1985 volcanic eruption in Colombia. Before becoming a photographer she graduated from nursing school.

Skeeter Hagler
American/Dallas, Texas
The 1980 Pulitzer Prize winner for feature photography, Hagler has worked for the *Dallas Times Herald* for the past 12 years. After receiving his B.A. in architecture from the University of Texas in 1971, Hagler turned to photojournalism as a full-time career. Since then he has won many state and national awards.

Al Harvey
Canadian/Vancouver, British Columbia
Al Harvey has been an audiovisual photographer for the past decade. His style tends to be cinematic, often seasoned with the surreal.

David Alan Harvey
American/Washington, D.C.
Harvey's assignments for *National Geographic* in the past 12 years have included Kampuchea, Honduras, Grenada, Mayan ruins, Spain and the Arctic. In 1978 Harvey was named Magazine Photographer of the Year by the National Press Photographers Association.

Gregory Heisler
American/New York, New York
Heisler has contributed covers and cover stories to *Life, Fortune, Time, Esquire, Connoisseur, Money, Business Week* and *The New York Times Magazine* and has photographed for corporate publications and advertising. He produced the last two performance books for the American Ballet Theatre.

Andy Hernandez
Filipino/Quezon City
Hernandez graduated with a degree in fine arts and entered photojournalism at the age of 23 as chief photographer of the Associated Press Manila bureau. He worked with AP for four years during which time he covered Southeast Asia and won many local awards. He is associated with Sygma Photos.

Francois Hers
Belgian/Paris
After studying architecture, Hers decided to devote his career to photography and reporting. He has published two books, *Interiors* and *Recit,* which won the 1983 Prix Nadar. In 1983 he was nominated artistic director of the Mission Photographique of DATAR.

Volker Hinz
German/New York, New York
For the last 12 years Hinz has been a staff photographer for *Stern* magazine, and he has been based in New York since 1978. The winner of many honors, he has traveled the world on assignments, and he has had one-man and group shows in Germany and the U.S.

Life magazine 1980

Ethan Hoffman
American/New York, New York
Hoffman is an internationally recognized photojournalist who has recently completed photo essays in Japan for *Life, Fortune, The New York Times Magazine* and *Connoisseur.* His work has appeared in major magazines around the world and Time-Life Books is publishing a book of his work on Japan. He is president of Archive Photos.

Eikoh Hosoe
Japanese/Tokyo
Winner of many awards for photography and internationally recognized for his photographs of Hiroshima, Hosoe is professor of photography at the Tokyo Institute of Polytechnics. He has exhibited all over the world, and his work is part of many museum collections. His books include *Ordeal by Roses*, *Man and Woman* and *Kamaitachi*.

Francoise Huguier
French/Paris
A frequent visitor to Asia, Huguier's photographs of China, Hong Kong and Japan have appeared in many magazines and newspapers. She also works as a fashion photographer for *Bazaar* and *Liberation*. Her work has been exhibited widely in France and throughout Europe. She is a member of the VU agency.

Graciela Iturbide
Mexico   1975

Graciela Iturbide
Mexican/Mexico City
Iturbide uses her camera to capture poetry in life. She has published two books in Mexico and has exhibited her work in Paris, Zurich and America.

Chris Johns
American/Seattle, Washington
Johns is currently a contract photographer with the National Geographic Society. In 1979 he was named Newspaper Photographer of the Year.

Lynn Johnson
American/Pittsburgh, Pennsylvania
As a contract photographer for Black Star since 1982, Johnson has shot for *Life*, *Newsweek*, *Forbes* and *Fortune*. Earlier she spent seven years as a staff photographer for the *Pittsburgh Press*, during which time she won seven Golden Quill awards. In 1984 she received a Robert F. Kennedy World Understanding Award, and in 1985 she won a World Press Photo Award.

Frank Johnston
American/Washington, D.C.
Johnston began his career with United Press International covering stories such as John F. Kennedy's assassination and the Vietnam War. He then joined *The Washington Post*, where he covers national news. A three-time winner of the White House News Photographers Association Photographer of the Year award, Johnston has won many other awards as well. In 1983 he won an Alicia Patterson fellowship to cover the social and economic changes in America.

Peter Jordan
British/London
After years of covering events in Africa for *Newsweek*, Associated Press and Fleet Street papers, Jordan joined *Time* magazine in 1978 and traveled to more than 30 African countries on assignment. In 1981 he moved back to London and has been traveling with Prime Minister Margaret Thatcher. He won the Olivier Rebbot Award in 1983 for his coverage in Beirut and Thatcher's election campaign.

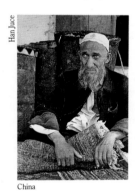
Han Juce
China

Han Juce
Chinese/Beijing
After graduating from the photography department of Chang Chun Cinema College, Juce was assigned as a staff photographer for Xinhua News Agency. He has also served as a picture editor and has traveled extensively in China and overseas.

Shelly Katz
American/Dallas, Texas
Katz sold his first pictures to the *New York Daily News* when he was 12 years old. A *Time* contract photographer, Katz has lived in Dallas since 1965. His assignments have ranged from the space program to presidential campaigns. He is represented by the Black Star agency.

Alain Keler
French/Paris
Keler won the 1986 World Press Photo first prize in the nature series. He is a Sygma photographer whose coverage of events such as the revolution in Iran, the civil war in El Salvador and strikes in Poland appears in *Time*, *Newsweek* and *Paris-Match*, among others.

Robb Kendrick
American/Houston, Texas
Kendrick has freelanced for *Forbes*, *Fortune*, *U.S. News and World Report* and *GEO* while working his way through East Texas State University. In the summer of 1986 he worked as a photographer in *National Geographic's* internship program.

David Hume Kennerly
Egypt   1978

David Hume Kennerly
American/Los Angeles, California
Winner of the Pulitzer Prize for his feature photography in Vietnam, Kennerly was also awarded the Overseas Press Club's Olivier Rebbot Award in 1986. Kennerly is a *Time* contract photographer who took a two-and-one-half year leave to serve as personal photographer to President Gerald Ford. The author of *Shooter*, he is currently producing and directing movies in Los Angeles.

Douglas Kirkland
Los Angeles   1962

Douglas Kirkland
Canadian/Los Angeles, California
Kirkland is one of the world's best known glamour and personality photographers. Twenty-five years in the business has included camera work with Marilyn Monroe, Judy Garland, Barbra Streisand and Christie Brinkley. He was one of the founding members of Contact Press Images and currently works with Sygma Photos.

Koo Bohn-Chang
Korean/Seoul
In 1975 Koo received a degree in business administration from Yon-Sei University in Seoul, and in 1985 he received a diploma in communication and photo design from the Fachhochschule Hamburg. He is a foreign correspondent of the Deutsche Gesellschaft fur Fotografie and has exhibited his work in Korea and Germany.

Sara Krulwich
American/New York, New York
Krulwich grew up in New York City, and for the last seven years has worked for her hometown paper, *The New York Times*. As a staff photographer, she has covered everything from parades to politics with time out for food, fashion and fires. Her most recent long-term project was Geraldine Ferraro's vice presidential campaign.

Hiroji Kubota
Japanese/Tokyo
In 1970 Kubota received the first Kodansha Publishing Culture Award, given by Japan's largest publishing house. He has produced many articles on Asia for the world's press, and in 1981 he was selected as the Japanese Photographer of the Year. Kubota's extensive work in Burma and China has resulted in a series of award-winning books. He is affiliated with Magnum Photos.

Kaku Kurita
Japanese/Tokyo
Kurita began his career as a commercial photographer, and in 1964 turned to photojournalism. Currently one of Japan's most successful international photojournalists, he works for *Time*, *The New York Times*, *Fortune*, *Forbes*, *Newsweek*, *Paris-Match*, *Figaro*, *Le Point* and *Stern*. He has been with Gamma in Tokyo for 12 years.

Jean-Pierre Laffont
French/New York, New York
Laffont attended the prestigious School of Graphic Arts in Vevey, Switzerland, prior to serving in the French Army in Algeria in the early 1960s. He has served as the New York correspondent for Reporters Associates and Gamma Press Images. Since 1973 he has been a partner of the Sygma Photo Agency. His work appears regularly in the world's leading news magazines.

Daniel Laine
French/Paris
A professional photographer for ten years, Laine started as a freelancer for *Liberation* and has worked for *Partir* and *Grand Reportages* doing travel stories on South America and Africa. He was a correspondent in Western and Central Africa for Agence France Presse, and since 1981 he has been a staff photographer for *Actuel*.

Xavier Lambours
Cannes   1983

Xavier Lambours
French/Paris
A specialist in portraits of celebrities, Lambours published a book on movie actors, *Cinemonde*, in 1983. He has also exhibited his portraits of politicians in France and throughout Europe. His work appears in *Liberation*, *Le Monde* and many magazines throughout Europe. He is a member of the VU agency.

Governor Richard Lamm
American/Denver, Colorado
Known for his outspoken stances on a variety of issues, Lamm became Governor of Colorado in 1975. He has written five books and in 1985 he won the *Christian Science Monitor's* "Peace 2010" essay competition. *A Day in the Life of America* was his first professional photography assignment.

Jacques Langevin
French/Paris
After studying photography, Langevin spent six years with Associated Press in Paris. He is a news photographer who currently works with Sygma.

Brian Lanker
American/Eugene, Oregon
The winner of a 1983 Pulitzer Prize and a 1984 World Press Photo first place award, Lanker has worked for several newspapers, including the *Eugene Register Guard*. His work also appears in *Sports Illustrated* and *Life*.

Frans Lanting
Dutch/Santa Cruz, California
Lanting's work appears in *National Geographic*, *GEO*, *Life* and for the National Wildlife Federation. He has been honored by the Association of Magazine Photographers, the Pictures of the Year competition and World Press Photos.

Sarah Leen
American/Philadelphia, Pennsylvania
A graduate of the University of Missouri, Leen has been on the staff of *The Philadelphia Inquirer* for four years covering stories in Monaco, Lebanon and South Africa. In 1986 she received an honorable mention in the Robert F. Kennedy awards for her story on Alzheimer's disease.

Andy Levin
American/New York, New York
Levin is a photojournalist whose essay on a Nebraska farm family for *Life* won top magazine division honors in the National Press Photographers Association Pictures of the Year competition in 1986. In 1985 Levin's essay on the Statue of Liberty for *Discover/National Geographic* won similar honors. He is a frequent contributor to *People*, *Parade* and *Signature*.

Barry Lewis
British/London
With an M.A. from the Royal College of Art, Lewis is a founding member of the Network agency. He works internationally for magazines such as *Time, The Sunday Times* (London), *The Observer* and *GEO*.

R. Ian Lloyd
Canadian/Singapore
Lloyd lives and works in Singapore producing books, audio visuals and videos on travel-related subjects. He has recently completed books on Bangkok, Hong Kong, Bali and Singapore as well as two books on architecture and one on aerial photography. His work also appears in *Time, Newsweek, GEO* and *Fortune*.

Gerd Ludwig
German/New York, New York
A founding member of the Visum Photo Agency in Hamburg, Ludwig is a regular contributor to *GEO, Life, Zeit Magazin, Stern, Fortune* and other magazines. He is a member of Deutsche Gesellschaft fur Fotografie. On May 4, 1986, he married Dana Fineman (see above). Two hundred of the world's best photojournalists covered the wedding.

Jay Maisel
American/New York, New York
One of the world's most sought-after photographers, Maisel's work appears regularly in magazines, advertisements and corporate publications. His color prints are included in numerous corporate and private collections. He received the Outstanding Achievement in Photography Award in 1978 and the Newhouse Citation from Syracuse University in 1979.

Pascal Maitre
French/Paris
Maitre has photographed conflicts the world over and has published his work in *GEO, Epoca* and *Figaro*. In 1985 he published a book on Zaire and in 1986 he won a World Press Photo award for his work in Iran. He is associated with Gamma in Paris.

Mary Ellen Mark
American/New York, New York
The winner of numerous awards and grants, Mark has exhibited and published her work the world over. In 1985 she won the Robert F. Kennedy Award and in 1986, the Phillipe Halsman Award for Photojournalism from the American Society of Magazine Photographers. Her work appears regularly in *Life, The Sunday Times* (London) *Stern, Vanity Fair* and *The New York Times*.

John Marmaras
Australian/Sydney
Marmaras has worked on assignment for magazines such as *Fortune, GEO, Time, Sports Illustrated, The Sunday Times* (London) and *The New York Times Magazine*. After 8 years in London and 13 years in New York, he is now based in Sydney doing magazine and corporate/industrial photography.

A Day in the Life of Australia   1981

Stephanie Maze
American/Washington, D.C.
Since 1979 Maze has been a freelance photographer for *National Geographic* and has worked in the U.S., Mexico, Spain, Portugal, Costa Rica, Puerto Rico and Brazil. She has covered three Olympic Games, and in 1985, won a first-place prize from the White House Press Photographers Association.

Linda McConnell
American/Denver, Colorado
A staff photographer for the *Rocky Mountain News*, McConnell was nominated in 1985 for a Pulitzer Prize and won the Helen Carringer Award and a citation from the Robert F. Kennedy awards.

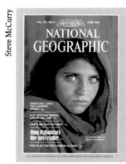
National Geographic   1985

Steve McCurry
American/New York, New York
In 1986 McCurry won four first-place awards in the World Press Photo Contest, one for his book, *The Imperial Way*. A freelance photographer for *National Geographic*, he has also won a Robert Capa Gold Medal and the 1984 Photographer of the Year Award from the National Press Photographers Association. He is associated with Magnum Photos.

Joe McNally
American/New York, New York
McNally is a contract photographer with *Sports Illustrated* and works regularly for *Life, Time, Esquire, Fortune, The Observer, GEO* and *Parade*.

Wally McNamee
American/Washington, D.C.
McNamee has been a photographer for 30 years with the USMC, *The Washington Post* and, since 1968, *Newsweek*. He is a four-time winner of the White House News Photographer Association Photographer of the Year Award and has also won several New York Art Directors' Club citations.

Dilip Mehta
Canadian/Toronto
An internationally known photojournalist, Mehta is a member of Contact Press Images. His work has appeared in *Time, Newsweek, GEO, Bunte, Paris-Match* and *The New York Times*. He has received gold medals from the World Press Association for his coverage of the Bhopal tragedy and for a feature on Rajiv Gandhi, prime minister of India.

Rudi Meisel
German/Hamburg
Meisel is a founding member of Visum, one of West Germany's top agencies. Since 1975 his work has appeared in *Zeit Magazin, Art, Der Spiegel, Stern, Time, Life* and *GEO*. He has won numerous awards and is currently working on photo projects in both East and West Germany.

Pennsylvania   1985

Michael Melford
American/New York, New York
Melford has photographed covers and feature stories for *Life, Newsweek, Connoisseur, New York* and *GEO*. He has won numerous awards for his editorial and annual report photography. As a result of his work on *A Day in the Life of Japan*, his work appeared in a one-man exhibit in the town he photographed, Kanazawa.

Doug Menuez
American/San Francisco, California
Currently on contract to *USA Today* covering the Northwest, Menuez is a member of the Picture Group agency. After graduating from San Francisco State University, he worked as a studio assistant and spent four years working for a variety of newspapers. His freelance work appears in *Time, Newsweek, U.S. News and World Report, Forbes* and *Business Week*.

Claus C. Meyer
Brazilian/Rio de Janeiro
The winner of many prizes and awards, Meyer was selected in 1985 by Communication World as one of the top ten annual report photographers in the world. His color work has been recognized by Kodak and Nikon, and in 1981 he won a Nikon International Great Prize. He has published several books on Brazil.

Maddy Miller
American/New York, New York
Currently assistant photo editor of *People*, Miller has worked at *Look* and *Us* and has freelanced for many major magazines. She has also worked as a photographer for MADRE, an organization involved with the women and children of Nicaragua.

Brian Milne
Canadian/Toronto
For the past two years, Milne has been working on a book about the world's longest highway, the TransCanada. In 1984 his *Equinox* cover was selected for the Communication Arts Annual. His work has appeared in *National Geographic, Audubon* and *Das Tier*. Milne is a founding member of Canada's First Light Associated Photographers.

Yan Morvan
French/Paris
In 1983 Morvan won a special citation from the Robert Capa awards for work done in Lebanon. He has been a freelance photographer for *Liberation, Figaro* and *Newsweek* and is associated with Sipa/Special Features.

Carl Mydans
American/Larchmont, New York
Mydans began his distinguished career in the 1930s as a reporter for *American Banker*. He worked for *Life* for 36 years. While covering WWII in the Pacific, he was a prisoner of war in the Philippines and China in 1942–43. He also covered the wars in Korea and Vietnam. Since 1972 Mydans has been a photographer for *Time*. His books include *More Than Meets the Eye, The Violent Peace* and *Carl Mydans, Photojournalist*. In 1960 he received an honorary doctorate from Boston University.

Matthew Naythons
American/San Francisco, California
A working photojournalist and physician, Naythons has spent most of his career alternating between photo coverage of world events and emergency-room duty in San Francisco. In 1979 he founded an emergency medical team to care for Cambodian and Thai refugees. His photographic work appears regularly in major magazines.

Andy Nelson
American/Manhattan, Kansas
A full-time photojournalism student at Kansas State University, Nelson has interned at *The Kansas City Star* and *The Denver Post*. In 1985 he placed second in the College Photographer of the Year contest.

Chris Niedenthal
British/Warsaw
The only Western photographer living and working in Poland, Niedenthal has witnessed and photographed Poland's contemporary history since 1973. His coverage of this period has appeared in *Stern, GEO* and *Newsweek*. He has also contributed photographs to many books on Poland. In 1985 he became a contract photographer for *Time*.

Moscow   1977

Alain Nogues
French/Paris
A photojournalist since 1964, Nogues' assignments have taken him to over 20 countries in Africa, the Middle East, Asia and South America. He won second prize in the 1985 World Press Photo competition for people in the news, and his work appears regularly in the world's leading news magazines. He is a co-founder and staff member of Sygma Photo Agency.

Kazuyoshi Nomachi
Japanese/Tokyo
Nomachi began freelancing in 1971 and since then has made several trips to North Africa and the Sinai. His books, *Sahara* and *Sinai*, have been published in five languages. He has also published books on the Nile and a second book on the Sahara won Japan's Ken Domon Prize.

Seny Norasingh
Laotian/Raleigh, North Carolina
Named North Carolina News Photographer of the Year in 1980 and 1982, Norasingh has been on the staffs of *The Raleigh News and Observer, The Gastonia Gazette* and *The Daily Advance*.

Koni Nordmann
Swiss/Zurich
Nordmann studied at the International Center of Photography in New York before returning to Zurich where he works for many major Swiss publications. He is associated with Contact Press Images and has recently completed assignments on the Statue of Liberty and on the opera singer Simon Estes. In 1985 he received a grant to work on a photo essay about his own basic training in the Swiss Army.

A Day in the Life of Canada   1984

Michael O'Brien
American/New York, New York
A native of Memphis, Tennessee, O'Brien began his career at the *Miami News* where his work was recognized with two RFK journalism awards for outstanding coverage of the disadvantaged. His work now appears frequently in *Life, GEO* and other magazines.

Richard Olsenius
American/Wayzata, Minnesota
Olsenius left the *Minneapolis Tribune* in 1981 to begin his own publishing/photography business, and he is currently preparing MIDWEST 1987, a black-and-white calendar. He has been honored for his news photography and for his film work.

Pablo Ortiz Monasterio
Mexican/Mexico City
Ortiz Monasterio studied economics in Mexico City and photography in London. He has published two books, *Los Pueblos del Viento* and *Testigos Y Comices*, and has exhibited in Paris, London and Mexico.

Graeme Outerbridge
Bermudan/Hamilton
Named the 1985 Young Outstanding Person of the Year in Bermuda, Outerbridge has exhibited his work in New York, Washington, D.C., London, Boston and Helsinki and has appeared in *Vogue* and *The New Yorker*, among others. He published *Bermuda Abstracts* and is working on a book about bridges.

Daniele Pellegrini
Italian/Milan
The son of a photojournalist, Pellegrini has been a freelance photographer since 1967. From 1976 to 1979 he documented "A truck around the world" for which he drove a heavy duty truck 115,000 miles across Europe, Asia, Africa and the Americas. He published a book about his travels and is currently director of photography for AQUA, a new Italian magazine.

Mark Peters
Zimbabwean/Johannesburg
Named South African Press Photographer of the Year and a Nikon prize winner, Peters has covered all of the African countries for *Newsweek* and newspapers around the world. His photographs of South Africa appear regularly in *The New York Times* and *Newsweek*.

Bill Pierce
American/New York, New York
A Princeton graduate, Pierce won the 1983 Overseas Press Club Olivier Rebbot Award. His work appears in major international publications such as *Time, Life, Paris-Match, The New York Times Magazine* and *Stern*.

Mario Pignata-Monti
Argentine/Paris
After completing graduate studies in animal genetics in Paris, Pignata-Monti turned his attention to full-time photojournalism. He has covered assignments in Argentina and around the world for *Time, Paris-Match* and *Stern*, and he recently completed a year in New York on a fellowship from the International Center of Photography.

Christopher Pillitz
Argentine/London
A self-taught photojournalist, Pillitz has traveled the world working for numerous publications including *The Observer, The Sunday Times Magazine* (London), *Newsweek, Time-Life, Vogue* and *Elle*. He has been on assignment in Vietnam, Argentina, East Africa, Haiti and Western Europe.

Jim Preston
American/Denver, Colorado
For ten years Preston was a Navy photographer, and in 1981 he was named Military Photographer of the Year. Since 1982 he has been a staff photographer for *The Denver Post*, and in 1983 he won a National Press Photographers Association Award for his coverage of Honduras.

Larry Price
American/Philadelphia, Pennsylvania
Two-time Pulitzer Prize winner and currently the director of photography for *The Philadelphia Inquirer's* Sunday magazine, Price has also worked for the *El Paso Times* and the *Fort Worth Star-Telegram*. His many awards include honors from the Overseas Press Club, World Press Photo awards and the National Press Photographers Association.

Jake Rajs
American/New York, New York
A frequent contributor to *Life, Esquire, Omni, Travel and Leisure* and *GEO*, Rajs has exhibited his work around the world and is represented in the permanent collections of museums and corporations. His book, *Manhattan, An Island in Focus*, sold out its first edition.

President Ronald Reagan
American/Washington, D.C.
Before turning to politics, Reagan had a long and successful career as a film actor. Reagan was governor of California and has served as President of the United States since 1981. To date, he has won no major awards as a photojournalist.

Eli Reed
American/New York, New York
A 1982-83 Nieman Fellow at Harvard, Reed won the 1985 Overseas Press Club Award and the World Understanding Award for his work on Central America. He is currently working on a book about the conditions of blacks in North America 20 years after the civil rights movement.

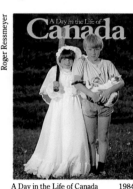
A Day in the Life of Canada   1984

Roger Ressmeyer
American/San Francisco, California
A Yale graduate, Ressmeyer is a freelancer whose work has appeared in *Time, People, Newsweek, Fortune* and *Life*. His specialties include portraiture, fashion and high technology.

REZA
Iranian/Paris
REZA began his career as a photojournalist during the 1978 Iranian revolution. He covered the American hostage crisis, the Kurdistan War and the Iran-Iraq War. In 1981 he was exiled to Paris and has since covered the world for major international magazines. He is a contract photographer for *Time*.

Jim Richardson
American/Denver, Colorado
Currently a special projects photographer for *The Denver Post*, Richardson has published essays from his work on his native state of Kansas in *Life, American Photographer* and *Country Journal*. He has achieved special recognition in the World Understanding Award in 1975, 1976 and 1977.

Steve Ringman
American/San Francisco, California
Two-time winner of both the NPPA Newspaper Photographer of the Year Award and the Bay Area Press Photographers' Photographer of the Year Award, Ringman is a staff photographer for the *San Francisco Chronicle*. Known for his compassionate coverage of people, he shot one of the first photo essays on AIDS.

Sophie Ristelhueber
French/Paris
After receiving a master's degree in literature from the Sorbonne, Ristelhueber worked as an editor. In 1979 she began her work as a photographer and joined the Rapho agency that same year. She won the award of the Societe Francaise de Photographie in 1985 for her book *Beirut/Photographs*.

Francois Robert
Swiss/Chicago, Illinois
Robert is a freelance photographer who shoots annual reports and corporate brochures for Fortune 500 companies in the U.S. and overseas. He has had several one-man and group shows internationally and is working on a book titled *Before-After*.

Art Rogers
American/Point Reyes, California
The winner of a 1986 Guggenheim Fellowship for his Point Reyes Family Album project, Rogers has exhibited his work widely. He has taught at the San Francisco Art Institute and also works in corporate and advertising photography.

Galen Rowell
American/Albany, California
Rowell is one of the world's outstanding environmental photojournalists. His work has appeared in *National Geographic, Outside, Audubon, Sierra* and *Sports Illustrated*. He has traveled widely throughout the U.S., Asia, Africa and the South Pacific in the course of his assignments.

April Saul
American/Philadelphia, Pennsylvania
Twice named Pennsylvania's Photographer of the Year, Saul became the first recipient of the National Press Photographers Association/Nikon sabbatical grant for her photographs of refugees in America. She has received many awards for her picture stories and is currently a staff photographer at *The Philadelphia Inquirer*.

Miami   1985

Debra Schulke
American/Miami, Florida
Schulke's assignments have ranged from NASA's space shuttle and its astronauts to *Miami Vice* star Don Johnson. Established as a fine arts photographer, her work appears regularly in *Life, Stern, Smithsonian* and *Bunte*.

Flip Schulke
American/Miami, Florida
For 35 years Schulke has been a freelance photojournalist associated with Black Star. He has won many awards internationally and has often served as a judge for photography competitions. His work has appeared in *Life, Stern, Smithsonian* and *The London Telegraph Magazine*.

Michael Shayegani
Iranian/Strasbourg
Shayegani moved to the U.S. from Iran in 1969 and at the age of 14 borrowed his father's Rolleiflex and began to pursue his interest in photography. Once an assistant to glamour photographer Douglas Kirkland, he is now starting a commercial photography business.

Vladimir Sichov
Stateless/Paris
Sichov left the U.S.S.R. in 1979 and since then his work has appeared internationally. He is a contract photographer for French *Vogue* and has published two books of photographs.

Hans Silvester
German/Paris
Born in Germany, Silvester has lived in France since 1961. His work appears most frequently in *GEO*, but his picture stories appear in many major international magazines. He has published 15 books.

Bill Simpkins
Canadian/Calgary, Alberta
Simpkins worked for the *Calgary Herald* for 14 years and is now employed in the public affairs department of Petro-Canada. His work has appeared in several magazines, and he has published a book on Alberta. He is the winner of a Canadian Press Award.

Tom Skudra
Canadian/Toronto, Ontario
Since 1967 Skudra has worked for a variety of clients in Canada and abroad, including the Canadian government, *MacLean's, Quest, The Globe and Mail* and Labatt's Breweries. He is a three-time winner of the Toronto Art Directors Club Award for Photojournalism.

Neal Slavin
American/New York, New York
The recipient of numerous awards, Slavin is published regularly in *The Sunday Times* (London), *Stern, GEO, Town & Country, Newsweek* and *Connoisseur*. His work has appeared in one-man and group shows and his latest book is *Britons*.

South Korea   1981

Ghana   1986

Rick Smolan
American/New York, New York
Co-director of the *A Day in the Life of America* project, Smolan is also responsible for *A Day in the Life of Australia* (1981), *A Day in the Life of Hawaii* (1983), *A Day in the Life of Canada* (1984) and *A Day in the Life of Japan* (1985). Prior to these extravaganzas, Smolan was a full-time photojournalist whose work appeared in major publications such as *Time* and *National Geographic*.

Jordi Socias
Spanish/Madrid
Since 1970 Socias has worked as a photographer for such leading Spanish publications as *El Pais* and *Cambio 16*. In 1979 he founded the COVER Photo Agency to bring together the best photojournalists in Spain. He has been a jury member for many photography competitions, including the World Press Photo contest in 1984.

James L. Stanfield
American/Washington, D.C.
Born into a family of newspaper photographers, Stanfield spent five years at *The Milwaukee Journal* before joining *National Geographic* in 1966. His assignments have taken him to 85 countries, and he is currently working on a piece on the Ottoman Empire and Suleiman the Magnificent. Three-time winner of the White House News Photographers Association News Photographer of the Year, he has exhibited his work at the Metropolitan Museum of Art in New York.

Andrew Stawicki
Polish/Toronto, Ontario
After working as a staff photographer in Frankfurt for *Bild Zeitung* and in Warsaw for *Swiatowid*, Stawicki joined *The Toronto Star* in 1983. He has won several prizes in Poland and Holland and has exhibited his work in Poland and Canada.

George Steinmetz
American/San Francisco, California
A graduate of Stanford University in geophysics, Steinmetz dropped out to spend two-and-one-half years hitchhiking through more than 20 African countries. His work appears regularly in *Fortune, Forbes, Business Week, Mother Jones* and *California* magazine.

Peter Stocker
American/Lawrence, Kansas
A film studies major at the University of Kansas, Stocker is planning a photographic essay on Australian filmmaking. He has been an oarsman for four years and has focused most of his photography on the people and sport of crew.

William Strode
American/Prospect, Kentucky
Strode has traveled the world on assignment for *Time, Life, Fortune, GEO, National Geographic* and *Stern*. He is the author of ten books and the winner of many awards, including Newspaper Photographer of the Year and Newspaper Magazine Picture Editor of the Year.

Anthony Suau
American/New York, New York
Winner of the Pulitzer Prize in feature photography in 1984, Suau has worked for *The Denver Post* and the *Chicago Sun-Times*. In 1986 he was named the most promising photographer under the age of 30 by the International Center of Photography. He is currently a contract photographer for Black Star.

Michel Szulc Krzyzanowski
Dutch/Amsterdam
Szulc Krzyzanowski works both as a photojournalist and art photographer. His work has appeared in the Dutch weekly *Nieuwe Revu* and is in the collection of a variety of museums including the Museum of Modern Art in New York, the Art Institute in Chicago and the Stedelijk Museum in Amsterdam.

Bruce Talamon
American/Los Angeles, California
In 1984 Talamon was a contract photographer for *Time* covering Jesse Jackson during the U.S. presidential primary and election campaigns. He is currently working as a still photographer on motion picture sets and creating special documentary projects for magazines.

Patrick Tehan
American/Santa Ana, California
In 1981 Tehan was named as a regional Photographer of the Year by the National Press Photographers Association. He is currently on the staff of *The Orange County Register* in Santa Ana, California.

Tomasz Tomaszewski
Polish/Warsaw
Tomaszewski's work appears in international publications such as *Stern, Paris-Match* and *La Vie*. His photographs have also appeared in exhibits in Poland and Paris. He is the photography editor of *Przeglad Katolicki* and a regular contributor to *Solidarity Weekly*.

David Turnley
American/Detroit, Michigan
The winner of many awards, Turnley has been a *Detroit Free Press* staff photographer since 1980. He has been recognized for his work on South Africa, and in 1986 he won three World Press Photo awards including the Oscar Barnack Award for a series on daily life in South Africa. In 1986 he also won the Canon Essayist Award and the Overseas Press Club Award for Best Newspaper and Wire Service Photo-Reporting for his South Africa coverage.

Peter Turnley
American/Paris
Turnley studied at the University of Michigan, the Sorbonne and the Institut d'Etudes Politiques before becoming a photographer for *Newsweek* covering Europe, U.S.S.R, North Africa and the Middle East. His work has appeared in magazines and newspapers internationally, and he has published a book, *A Food Lover's Guide to Paris*. He works with Rapho Photos in Paris.

Penny Tweedie
British/London
Tweedie is best known for her documentation of international social issues such as the Bangladesh refugees, the Indo-Pakistan war and the Arab/Israeli conflict. Her many grants and awards include those from the British Arts Council and the Australian Arts Council.

A Day in the Life of Japan   1985

Neal Ulevich
American/Beijing
The Associated Press photo editor for China, Ulevich has spent 16 years in Asia covering a variety of stories, including the Vietnam War. He won the Pulitzer Prize for news photography in 1977 for photos of violent political upheaval in Thailand.

Burk Uzzle
American/St. David's, Pennsylvania
Uzzle has been a contract photographer for *Life* since 1962 and was a member of Magnum Photos. His work appears internationally and is in many museum collections. He is the author of *Burk Uzzle: Landscapes*.

Jerry Valente
American/New York, New York
Valente's honors and awards are all in his future. *A Day in the Life of America* was his first major assignment, and he did very well indeed.

John Vink
Belgian/Brussels
A member of VU in Paris, Vink has been a freelance photographer since 1971. His work appears in *Time, Le Monde* and *Liberation*, and he is currently involved with personal projects on Italy and the African Sahel. His photographs have appeared in 30 group and solo shows in Europe.

Patrick Ward
British/London
In 1975 Ward received a Kodak bursary which resulted in the publication of *Wish You Were Here—The English at Play*. Other publications include *Flags Flying*, a record of British Jubilee celebrations, and *The Bike Riders*, a study of motorcyclists.

Ron Watts
Canadian/Toronto
In 1985 Watts published *The Last of the Wild Horses*. He has covered Tibet, Australia, Kenya, France and Hawaii for *Forbes, Fortune, Saturday Night, Equinox* and *International Wildlife*, among others. He is a founding member of Canada's First Light Associated Photographers.

A Day in the Life of Hawaii   1985

Mark S. Wexler
American/New York, New York
Wexler travels the world as a photographer for a variety of editorial and corporate clients including *Time, Life, Fortune* and *GEO*. He won three World Press Photo Awards for his work on *A Day in the Life of Japan*.

John H. White
American/Chicago, Illinois
Winner of more than 200 awards, including a 1982 Pulitzer Prize, White bought his first camera for 50 cents and 10 bubble gum wrappers. The Pulitzer Prize board praised his consistently excellent work on a variety of subjects, and since 1978 he has been sharing his expertise with students at Columbia College in Chicago.

Joy Wolf
American/Tucson, Arizona
A freelance photographer since 1985, Wolf began her career working for *The Arizona Daily Star* and *The San Jose Mercury News*. Her work is in the collection of the Center for Creative Photography and has been published in national and international magazines and newspapers.

Adam Woolfitt
British/London
Since doing his first freelance assignment for *National Geographic* in 1966, Woolfitt has worked for major U.S. magazines such as *Fortune, Travel and Leisure* and *Connoisseur* and European publications such as the *London Telegraph Sunday Magazine* and *GEO*.

Michael S. Yamashita
American/Mendham, New Jersey
A regular contributor to *National Geographic* since 1979, Yamashita is also a contributing photographer to *Signature*. His advertising clients include Singapore Airlines, Nikon Cameras, Dai Nippon Printing Company, Nissan Motors and the Harvard Business School.

Ian Yeomans
British/London
Yeomans began his career as an assistant in a fashion studio and went on to become a staff photographer at *Queen* magazine and at *The London Sunday Times Magazine*. In 1981 he won first prize in color picture story category of the World Press Photo competition.

Franco Zecchin
Italian/Palermo
Zecchin has published his work in many Italian magazines and journals and has exhibited in Palermo, Milan, Amsterdam, London and Boston. He is well known for his documentation of the Sicilian Mafia.

Tom Zetterstrom
American/Canaan, Connecticut
Zetterstrom's *Faces of China* has been exhibited nationally and his portfolio *White Russia* is in the permanent collection of the Library of Congress. His photographs appear in *Aperture, Time-Life Photoyear, The New York Times, Village Voice* and *Quest*.

Friends, Advisors, and Consultants

Sue Abrams
Linda Sue Abrams
Nate Accardo
David Adams
Rick Adie
Alyssa Adkins
Edward Agundez
Dr. John Ahlhauser
George Ahmaogak
Tony Alcazr
Charles Alcott
Ricardo E. Allen
Woody Allen
Daine Allman
Art Altenbe
Don Amano
Joe American Horse
Jo Amsterdam
Tom Anderson
Gregory P. Andorfer
Susan Andrews
Don Armstrong
Ann Arnold
Leslie Arnold
Herb Ascherman
Peggy Atkinson
Father Bob Aubrey
Tom Babcock
Alan Baer
Ed S. Bailey
Janice Bain
Senator Howard Baker
Billy Baker
Diane Ball
Beth Bangor
Len Banks
Susan Barnes-Gelt
Dale & Vonnie Barr
Hence & Thelma Barrow
Joe Bator
Clare Bavis
Errol Beauchamp
Bob Beck
Susan Beckmann
Doug Bedell
John Bedford-Lloyd
Ken Behnke
David Bell
Tom Bell
Tom Bender
K.C. & Becky Benson
Tim Berg
Leo Berg, Jr.
Gussie Bergerman
Bill Bergstrom
Bob Beyn
Larry & Sandy Bigos
Michael Binks
Miriam Birch
Alewyn Birch
Diane Birk
Charlotte Black Elk
Brian Blackburn
Roberta Blackgoat
Dierdre Blackwood
Jim Blair
Raymond Bleesz
Gloria Blissmore
Marty Bloedsoe
Tommy Boettcher
Bruce Bohne
Bill Booher
Delmar Borer
Neal Bortz
Marty Bosttdorf
Tani Bova
Lynn Bower
Richard Bower
Jim Bradburn
Julian Bradshaw

Raina Breien
Pete Brent
Karen Breunig
Harvey Bridges
Andrea Bronsten
Ernie Brookins
Dottie Brown
Charles Brown
Sarah Brown
John & Judy Brush
Kim Bruyn
Caitlin Buchman
Buck Buchwack
David Buckley
David & Pat Buffam
Joe Bullard
Rena K. Bunn
Elwin Bunzli
John Buquoi
Chief Justice Warren Burger
Frank Burke
Jim Burnett
T. Burnett
Charlie Burnham
Mayor W. C. Burnley
Mrs. Joy Burns
Elsie Burrell
Chris Bush
Sean Callahan
Susan Campbell
Darren E. Cannard
Cornell Capa
Diane Marie Carbone
Debbie Carcanes
Glenn Cardwell
Mike Carlton
Jim Carrier
Richard Carter
Ovie Carter
Daniel Carver
Mr. & Mrs. Roy Carver
Tony Casale
Judge Jeffrey Cates
Arthur Cerre
Larry Chabot
Lawrence Chabot
Katie Chalfont
John Chalmers
Father Gregory Chamberlin
Vanessa Chase
Sylvia Chase
Andy Chase
Dan Chavez
Senator John Chernenko
Kip Cheroutes
Donna Chitwood
JudyAnn Christensen
Rob Christie
Albert Chu
Cheech
Katy & Cheese Chudacoff
Patty Cinelli
Jane Hamilton Cirigliano
Hon. Henry Cisneros
Jesse & Rhoda Claman
William P. Clark
Sarah Clark
Gary Clarke
Lt. Cdr. Steve Clawson
Gerald Clifford
Marg Clift
Ann Kelly Cohan
Daniel Cohen
Norman & Hannah Cohen
Rose Cohen
Gail Cohen
David & Mickey Colfax
Kathy Collins
Sharon Collins
Vicky Cominsky
Janine E. Conklin
Jim Conley
Ted Conover
Ann Cooke
Jack Corn
Anne Cornell
Rebecca Cornell
Lee Couch
Michael D. Cox
Sallie Sue Crawford
Major George Creach

Hondo Crouch
Rev. Delano Cunningham
Charles Cuny
Chris Curtis
Sal Cusomato
Georgiana Custino
S/Sgt. Joe D'Acunto
Dianne D'Agostino
Cheryl Dailey
Donald P. Dalrymple
Mark Daniels
John & Ellen Daniels
Bob Dannin
Brenna Davenport-Leigh
Robyn Davidson
Pat Davidson
Merlin Davidson
Kathy Davidson
Susan Davis
Bob Davis
Bob Davison
Nancy Dawson-Sauser
Joel Day
Ramon & Maria de la Luz Vasquez
Edwin Deal
Cliff Deeds
Capt. Phil Delaney
Rudy & Anne DeLeon
Bob Delisle
Mary Demos
Ray DeMoulin
Carol Dew
Diane Dickey
Phil Dickinson
Jim & Abi Dickson
William M. DiMascio
Walter Dods
Steve Donovan
Joan Dority
Bob Dorkson
Margo Patterson Doss
Linda Dougherty
Ken Doyle
O. Burch & Debbie Drake
Gayle & Gene Driskell
Natasha Driskell
Ray Duncan
Tom Duncan
Dale Dunn & Family
Gigi Dux
Lois Eagleton
Diane Earl
Suzy Earl
John Eberle
Fred Echeandia
Pat & Dennis Eddy
Paul & Diane Edman & Family
Anne Edmonson
Terry Eiler
Mark Eisen
Homer Ellis
Bill Ellzey
Jan Envall
Linda Erb
Nora L. Erickson
Elliott Erwitt
Ellen Erwitt
Dianne & Wayne Estep
Steve Ettlinger
Steve & Dana Evans
Alice Evans
Nancy Evans
Patrick Fahey
Barth Falkenberg
Mr. & Mrs. Joe Fallini
Robert Fast Horse
Sandy Felsenthal
Harlan Felt
Forrest Fenn
Curt Fentress
Mary C. Ferrell
Carol Fiederlein
Dr. Peter Fischer
Beverly Fisher
Dick Fleming
Viorel Florescu
Judith Fluck
Frank Folwell
Chris Forrest
Jim Forsythe
Mary Kay Forsythe

Diana & Fred Fortney
Dave Frum
Jerry & Laura Frye
Micheal Fryer
Ron Fundingsland
Bill Gallagher
Carl Ganter & Family
Jeanie Gargano
Richard Garnier
Sister Ninfa Garza
Steve & Ina May Gaskins
Charle Gasta
Jennifer Gavin
Doug Geeting
Scott Geffert
Christine George
Joan Gerig
Alan Gerstenberger
Lou Gerwitz
Craig Gietzen
Bill Gignac
Vince Gill
Rory Gillespie
Bill Giordano
Vicki Godbey
H.G. Godbey
Svenja Goldberg
Nancy Goldberg
Arlene Goldfischer
Suzanne Goldstein
Paul & Kim Goligoski
Dennis Goode
Sue Goodell
Ray Goodew
Dennis Gordon
Mrs. D. Gorton
Paul Gottlieb
Stan Gotwin
Petter Gould
Lt. June Green
Lovie Griffin
Thomas Grimshaw
Stanley Grover
Debbie Gunn
Gordon Gust
Phil Guthrie
Gypsy
Terry Haack
Joe Haas
Jim & Roni Hale
Pete & Rayna Hale
Don Haley
Bonnie Hall
Mike Hall
Bill Ham
Duane Hamann
Edward Hamb
Cindy Hamlin
Allen & Pam Hammond
Vernon & June Hammond
Joy Hampp
Pam Hanney
Dr. Thomas J. Hanson
Don Hanson
Gaylon Hanson & Family
Dr. Bob Harcharek
John Harding
Jim Harpster
Nick Harris
John Harte
Rick & Gail Harvotich
Michael Hatt
Larry Hatteburg
Charles M. Hauptman
Jim Havey
Bob Hayes
Laura Haynes
Patinson Hayton
James Healy Jr.
Francois Hebel
Don Heilman
Robert & Ginny Heinlein
Chibuya Heng
Christy Hengel
Charles Henle
Helen Henry
Stanley James Herd
S/Sgt. Rudi Hernandez
Tom Hexner
Father George Hickey
Deb Hickok

Linda Hidy
Randy Hinds
Elaine Hoffman
Ruedi Hoffman
Jay Holmayer
Eugene Hoover
Doug Hopfer
Ray & Gene Hopper
Victoria Horn
Richie Horowitz
Benny Horton
Dr. David Horton
Joe Houlihan
Toni House
Helen Houser
Philip & Julie Howard
Carla Hubbard
Harlan Hubbard
Harry & Sharon Huber
Nancy Huckabay
Alex Hudson
Cliff Hudson
Ronnie Hughes
Mark Humphries
John Hunsicker
Ray L. Hunt
Kathy Hurlihy
David Ige
Kathy Itta
Vern Iuppa
Bill Ivey
Dr. Allan Izumi & Family
Dr. Edith James
David Janello
Kenneth & Evelyn Janello
Patti Jay
Cary Jehl
Richard Jenks
Sam Jewett
Steve Jobs
Geraldine Johnson
Linda Johnson
Kelly Johnson
Greg Johnstone
Jeff Joiner
Eddie & Yvonne Jones
Mother Lorena Jones
Ken Jones
Robert Jones
Maureen Judge
Wayne Juneau
Jerry Jywin
Lajos Louis Kalmer
Marc Kaplan
Susan Kare
Rich & Deena Karlis
Dr. Amalia Katsigeanis
Marcie Katz
Diane Kay
Dave Keenan
Nancy Keene
Tom Kelley
Tim Kelly
Brian J. Kennedy
Julene Pepion Kennerly
Frank Kent
Hooper Kent
Russell Kerns
William D. Kesler
Bern Ketchum
Karen Kietzman
Kerry Kimler
Erin King
John King
Luella King
Lt. Col. Randal R. Kirchner
Yorie Kiriyama
Frances Kitching
Nada Klein
The Klein Family
Mr. & Mrs. Fred Knechel
Jennie Kopf
Jeannine Kopsa
Tom Korest
Barry Kough
Jeff Kravitz
The Kraybill Family
Dick Kreck
Greg Kroll
Henry Kronberg
Steve Krongard

m Kroth	Lura Nell Mitchell	Michael Phillips	Dick Seawall	Elizabeth Tyler
drew Kruger	Sherriff Buddy Mitchell	Bill Phillips	Jeff Selby	Art Tyra
ed Kuehl	Phillip Moffitt	Lymon Pierce	Nikki Seligman	Elroy Ubl
me Kuehnel	Irene Molera	Chris Pietsch	Lee Sentell	Martha Underwood
ark Kurlansky	Arthur Mont	Eric A. Pike	Kay Sexton	Della Van Heyst
ugh LaBere	Andrea Montoni	Jim Pirter	Ann Jennings Shackleford	Major James Vance
on Lamb	Larry Moore	Elizabeth Pope	Sean J. Shannon	Kevin Vandivier
ger Lambert	Marat Moore	Mike Potts	Chris Shannon	Frank Varney
overnor Richard Lamm	Peter D. Moore	Tim Powers	Ira Shapiro	Hon. Marcelino Varona
ll Lane	Bob Morehouse	Dave Price	W. Jim Shaw	Ramon & Maria Vasquez
am Lapp	Jill Morelli	Jan Prothro	Peter Shelton	Garth Vaughan
X. Larrabee	Richard Moreno	Marsha Prouse	Paul Shepard	Pamela Vessey
kiko Launois	Trudy Morgan	Paul Pruneau	Jim Shofstall	Mr. Vianoy
anne Lawrence	Todd Morgan	Pat & Sophie Pumpkin Seed	Paul Simon	Tina Vicini
ck Lawson	Kathy Morgan	Carol Putnam	Stanford Singer	Mrs. Vincyk
ster Maureen Leach, OSF	Perry Morgan	Lt. Cdr. Craig Quigley	Gerry Singer	Pat & Chris Vinton
eborah LeClear	Lowell & Becky Morgan	Elizabeth P. Quinn	Wayne Sinyella	Dean Vogelaar
hris Lee	Wayne Morris	Art Racine	The Sisto Family	George Vogt
cki S. Lee	Rod Morris	The Rae Family	Richard Sitts	Tom Voight
n Lee	Jeffrey Morse	Marbella Rael	Dr. Thomas Skinner	Allan & Bita Wade
ike Lennox	Capt. Craig Moser	Rob Raker	Joan Slafsky	Bob Wade
seph Lentini	John F. Motch	Jan Ralph	Shirley Sliwa	John Wagner
aren Lenzi	Carlton (Buddy) Mott	Barbara Rankin	Aaren Slom	Dr. Greg Wagner
chard Levick	Bruce Mowery	Pamela Rannals	Richard M. Smith	Loyd Waites
artin Levin	Robin Moyer	Gary Rarette	Doug Smith	Chris Waites
ndy & Evelyn Levine	Allison Muench	Colette Radcliffe	Jerry Smith	Dan Walgreen
mes & Lynn Levinson	Mark Mullen	Bob Rauker	Steve Smith	Sonia Walker
dy Jones Lewis	Deborah Munch	Jane Raymond	Temple Smith	Michael Wall
illiam Lewis	Lee Muntz	President Ronald Reagan	Marvin & Gloria Smolan	Ruth Walsh
onna Linder	Judge Francis T. Murphy	Jay & Lynn Reardon	Sandy Smolan	Sharon Walters
wight & Karen Lindquist	James E. Murphy	Joe Recknor	Marcos Solberg	Whitney Ward
bby Lindsay	Aleck & Lynne Myers	Ben Reddick	Grace Song	Simon Wartin
naron H. Linhardt	Naoka Nakamura	Judy Redlick	Christopher Sorce	Scott Waters
arbara Little	Lyle Nalivka	Roy Reed	Drake Sorey	Tom Watkin
homas Lloyd	Phil Nash	Gary Reed	Major Phil Soucy	Elva Weakley
usan Lloyd	Jamie Nathanson	Michael & Michele Reese	Peter Sparkman	Spider Webb
dward & Anne Lloyd	Edwin J. Neilson	Gary Regester	Larry Speakes	Robert W. Webb
r. & Mrs. Bill Lloyd	Roger Nelson	Arlene Reid	David Spear	Clay Webb
arry Locker	Susan Neumeir	John Reid	Dick Spinosi	John Weeks
ohn Loengard	The Nguyen Family	Les Reinsertson	Annie Sprinkle	Rock Weiss
ichard LoPinto	Marie Nichols	Ron Reisman	William Steamer	Andy Weisser
rry Lubenow	Rob Nordin	Steve Renfro	Jim Stockton	Bill Welch
ally & Jerry MacCartee	Jim Norgard	Turner Reuter, Jr.	Sammy T. Stone	Don Wells
arolyn Mack	Matt Norman	Harold Reynolds	Linda Story	Daniel Wenk
inny Maes	Paul Norton	Les Rich	Bruce G. Strand	Lee Wenneke
arol Mageehon	Jean-Jacques Noudet	Arlene & Bernard Richards	Tom & Cee Jay Stratton	Otto Werner
ck Mahoney	Chuck Novak	Kathy Richardson	Joe Strear	Richard West
Michael Mailer	Bob O'Connor	Bob Richins	Jerry Strobel	Francis Westfield
ne Malless	Patrick O'Driscoll	Karin Richmond	Tom Strongman	Kathleen Whalen
lfred Mandel	Dan O'Neil	Charlie Riedel	Sylvia, Ari & Mies Surdoval	Hon. Mark White
hom Marchionna	Roger O'Neil	Joan Rivers	Peter Sutch	Noelani & Rick Wittington
ernadine Marinelli	David O'Neil	Andy Roberts	Nancy Suttles	Hon. Sam Wilcots
oe Marquez	Laura Odgers	Phil "Zoom" Roberts	Ellen Swartz	Shirley Willard
armelita Marris	Bob Oerman	Kim Roberts	Rick Swig	Bud Williams
renda Marsh	Jan Olsen	Peggy Robertson	Jim Talik	Dr. Henry & Dorothea Williams
anice & Bobby Marshall	Sue Olson	James Robinson-Long	Karen Tandy	Ann Williams
Mary Ada Marshall	Paul & Mary Olson	The Rodriguez Family	Ronal Taniwaki	Gil P. Willis
Mike Marshall	Melvin One Cloud	Ray Rogers	Drew Tate	James. D. Wilson
Dan Maschoff	Leola One Feather	Joe Rotkowski & Family	Liz Tavitas	John Wilson & Family
Pat Masini	Yoko Ono	Judge Luis D. Rovira	Claire Taylor	Lee Winneke
im & Laura Maslon	Hon. Richard Opela	Edythe Rubin	Joan Teasdale	Matthew Winokur
Elizabeth Mason	Bill & Marion Orton	Joe Ruthkowski	Jack Terhar, Jr.	Susan Winston
Tad Masterson	Meg Page	Nola Safro	Ana Terraza	Vic Winter
Rosario Masul	K. Kenneth Paik	Mario Saikhon	Henrietta Terrazas	Mike Wohlfeld
Richard & Lucienne Matthews	John Painter	David Saltz	Mike Tharp	Dennis Wolcott
Larry & Joyce Mayer	Rusty Pallas	Marianne Samenko	Bob Thayer	Gary Wolf
Nancy McCoy	Ed Paradine	Kai Sanburn	The Boyd Bro's	Rick Wolf
Liz McCracken	Charles Park	Dave Sanders	Shirl Thomas	Mike Wolinski
Mark & Berta McDonnell	Dolly Parton	Elmo Sapwater	Sgt. Jodi Thomas	Nancy Woodhall
Pat McFerrin	Anne Pasque	Nancy Dawson Sausers	John Thomas	Joe Woods
Don & Pat McGill	Dow & Betty Patterson	Victoria Sayer	Chuck Thomson	Peter Workman
Quentin McGown IV	Jack Paul	Sonny & Karen Scalese	Candice Thornton	Simon Worrin
Major Jim McGuire	Ken Paul	Corey Scarbrough	Robin Thunder Horse	Nancy Wright
Dr. David McIntyre	Jeff Payne	Dick Schaap	Terry & Susan Tice	Rich Wright
Barbara McKay	Don & Gretchen Payne	Armin Scheider	Lee Tiger	Tim Wright
The McKinney Family	William Pekala	Steve Scheier	Anne C. Tobin	Donna & Allen Wurzbach
Jeff McLaughlin	Yumiko Penney	Thomas Schenck	Doug Todd	Larry Wyner
Tim McMahon	Paul Peregrine	Michael Schenker	Laurie Todd	David Wynne
Lt. Cdr. Trish McMillan	Walter Perkins	Fred Scherrer	Gerry Tomascelli	Jack Yewell
Karin McMillan	Elizabeth Perle	Cliff Schiappa	Mark Tomasch	Patty Young
Tom McPoyle	Irvin Perlstein	Dick Schlosberg	Ken Tonge	David Yudain
Jay Meisenhelder	Tim Perry	Bob Schmidt	Leo Toskin	Bernie Yuman
Brenda K. Melcher	Mildred Petefish	David Schneider	Gary Towne	Zack Zacinini
William D. Mellon	Randy Peters	Geoff Schneider	Bob Townsend	Lee Zaichik
Pat Metheny	Anne-Margrethe Petersen	Steve Schneider	David Travis	Bruce Zake
Carol Meyer	Tam Petersen & Family	Louise Schnick	Amy Treibeck	Ray Zemik
Hank Miller	Larry Peterson	Charlie Schreiner III	Ian Treibeck	Patricia Ziegler
Eric Miller	Tom & Jean Peterson	Della Schuller	Pat Treibeck	Chuck Zillo
Lt. Col. Mike Miller	The Peterson Family	Melissa Schumer	Katana Truluck	Julie Zirbel
Pam Miracle	Penny Phelps	Stephen W. Scott	George Tuck	Luetta Zook
Dave Mitchell	Lt. J.G. Phiole	Charles Scott	Karen Tuso	Eugene A. Zykov

Sponsors and Contributors

Major Sponsors
Eastman Kodak Company
Merrill Lynch & Co., Inc.
United Airlines
Nikon Inc.
The Hertz Corporation
Apple Computer, Inc.

Major Contributors
Banana Republic
British Airways
Brown Palace Hotel, Denver
C. W. Fentress & Associates
Cambridge Development Group
Denver Inn
Denver Public Schools
Embassy Suites Hotel, Denver
Fairmont Hotel, Denver
Holiday Inn, Denver
Image Labs
Kittredge Properties
KOA Radio 85
Marlowe's Restaurant
Marriott Hotel, Denver
Pallas Photo Lab, Inc.
Professional Travel Corp.
Radisson Hotel, Denver
Sheraton Denver Tech Center
Sill-Terhar Ford
The Burnsley Hotel, Denver
The Denver Partnership, Inc.
The Oxford Hotel, Denver

Contributors
AA/ACT, Inc.
Air France
Allright Colorado, Inc.
American Gymnastics Training
    Center
American Society of Magazine
    Photographers
Apollo Courier Systems, Inc.
ARCO Alaska
Associated Press
AT&T Information Systems
Balcar-Tekno
Bally's Park Place

Baron Aviation
Bethlehem Steel Corp.
Black Star Publishing
Boardman Youth Center
Butler Rents
Cabin Creek Health Association
Cairo Evening Citizen
California Dept. of Youth
    Authority
Camren Photographic Rental
CEAVCO
Center Copy
Chicago Tribune
Clarion Hotel
Cleveland Plain Dealer
Coldwell Banker Commercial
    Real Estate Services
Colorado National Bank of Denver
Colorado Visual Aids
Commander Submarine Force,
    U.S. Atlantic Fleet
Commander-in-Chief,
    U.S. Atlantic Fleet
Contact Press Images
Coopers & Lybrand
Copper Range Co.
Crystal Run School
Dallas Cowboys Football Club
Dallas, Texas, Police Department
Day, Webb and Taylor
Delta Queen Steam Boat Co.
Denver Art Director's Club
Denver Center for the
    Performing Arts
Denver Chamber of Commerce
Denver Post
Denver Public Schools
Department of the Army
Detroit Free Press
Dollywood
Dolphin Research Center
Driskell Hotel
Dworshak National Fish Hatchery
East Texas State University
Eastman Kodak Co., Denver
Eastman School of Music
Edgewater Office Products
Elliott School
Esalen, Big Sur
Esquire Magazine
Executive Helicopter
FBI School at Quantico
Federal Express Corp.
Fenn Art Galleries
Fieldcrest-Cannon Mills, Inc.
Flash Video Productions
Ford Motors

Frontier Nursing Service
Gallaudet College
General Motors
Gilchrist Lumber Co.
Graceland
GranTree Furniture Rental Corp.
Great Smokies National Park
Havey Productions
Hickory Grove Pork Farm
Hidden Valleys
Hyatt Regency Hotel
Immigration & Naturalization
    Services-Border Patrol
International Center of
    Photography
John Chalmer's Farm
K.C.H., Inc.
Kemper Military School
    and College
Ken Hansen Photographic, Inc.
Ken Lieberman Laboratories
Kohala Coast Resort Association
La Posada Hotel
LaJitas Inn
LaJitas Trading Post
Lane Technical High School
Latino Youth High School
Lewiston Morning Tribune
Liberation Magazine, Paris
Liberty Universtiy
Life Magazine
Lone Wolf Bar & Cafe
Los Angeles Indian Center
Los Angeles Police Department
LTV Steel Macazine
MacUser
Magnum Photos
Marillac House
MarkAir
Marriott Hotels, Chicago
Mauna Lani Bay Hotel
McDonalds, Denver
Memphis-in-May International
    Festival, Inc.
Mesquite Championship Rodeo
Milwaukee Sentinel
Mischer Corp.
Mustang Ranch
NASA, Ames, A.F.B.
NASA, Edwards, A.F.B.
National Archives
National Hot Rod Association
National Park Service, U.S.
Department of the Interior
Nautilus Fitness Centers of
    New Mexico
Saul S. Negreann, Inc.

New York Magazine
New York Stock Exchange, Inc.
Newsweek Magazine
NewVector Communications, Inc.
Nissan Motor Manufacturing
    Corp., U.S.A.
North Carolina School of Arts
Northrop Corp.
Norton
Ocean Reef Club
Odessa, Texas Bureau of Tourism
Office of the Governor, State of
    Colorado
Office of the Governor, State of
    Oklahoma
Office of the Governor, State of
    Texas
Oglebay Norton
Ohio University
OMNI Hotel
Operation PUSH
Oral Roberts University
Pabst Brewing Co.
Paramount Theatre
Parkland Hospital
Paul Werth Associates., Inc.
Peabody Hotel
Pencils
People Magazine
Petro-Canada
Photon Video Arcade
Pitchfork Ranch
Pitney Bowes, Denver
Plume Ltd.
Pontiac Motor Division
Popular Photography
Potlatch Corp.
Power Promotions
Prabhupada's Palace of Gold
Professional Business
    Resources, Inc.
Provine Flying Service, Inc.
RCA Records
Read-Poland Advertising
Red Fox Inn
Research Triangle Foundation
Retail Planning Associates
RJ Reynolds Tobacco Co.
RJR Nabisco, Inc.
S & W Classics
Seaworld
Silver Streak Square and Round
    Dancing Festival
Skyline Building Maintenance
Special Events, Inc.
Stapleton Plaza Hotel
Stern Magazine

Stock Imagery, Inc.
Stockton Post Office
Stryker Weiner Associates
Surfing Magazine
Sygma Photos
Telos Corp.
Texas Department of
    Correction
Texas Sesquicentennial
    Commission
Texas Wagon Train Association
The Citadel
The Communications Works, Inc.
The Concord Resort Hotel
The Great Peace March
The Groton School
The Honolulu Advertiser
The National Fitness Institute
The National Geographic Society
The Petroleum Club of Billings,
    Montana
The Spee Club
The Sunday Times (London)
The Volunteers of America
The White House
The Yellowstone Country Club
Time Magazine
Town Properties
Traverse City Record Eagle
U.S. Air Force, Edwards AFB
U.S. Coast Guard
U.S. Dept. of Energy, Hanford
    Nuclear Reservation
U.S. Naval Academy
U.S. Navy, Bangor Submarine
    Base, Bremerton
U.S. Supreme Court
U.S.S.R. Information
    Department
United Mine Workers of America
United Parcel Service, Rocky
    Mountain District
United Steelworkers
University of Houston
University of Indiana
University of Missouri
Varig Brazilian Airlines
Waites Transport, Inc.
Weyerhauser Corp., Springfield
White Water Express
Wind Waves & Wheels Surf Shop
Woodbine Corporation
Woodfin Camp Associates
WQED, Pittsburgh
Y O Ranch
YMCA of Metropolitan Denver
Youngstown Board of Education

Thank you to the People of America.